Take Back Your Pearls

By Lorie Kay

WTL INTERNATIONAL

TAKE BACK YOUR PEARLS

Copyright © 2023 Lorie Kay

Cover artwork by Cutie Fruity by WTL International

All rights reserved. No part of this publication may be reproduced in any form or by any electronic or mechanical means, including information storage and material systems, except in the case of brief quotations embodied in critical articles or reviews, without permission in writing from its publisher,
WTL International.

Published by
WTL International
930 North Park Drive
P.O. Box 33049
Brampton, Ontario
L6S 6A7 Canada
www.wtlipublishing.com

978-1-778310-36-2

Printed in the U.S.A.

Pearls

Pearls are precious and beautiful, just like the soul of a woman. For some reason, despite other imagery out there, it has always been pearls that make me think of God's beauty in us.

The Bible tells us in Matthew 7:6 not to throw our pearls before swine. In other words, do not give away what is precious to someone or something undeserving. But what if we didn't give it away? What if our pearls were stolen? I have felt that what was precious to me was ripped away, cruelly taken against my will. Where did that leave me?

I was sexually abused by my father for my entire childhood. The girl in me, and then the young woman in me, wanted to see sex as something romantic and beautiful. But the reality of my world showed it to be ugly, disgusting, and painful. The precious gift that I was supposed to give to my husband someday was defiled, dragged through the sewer, ruined. My pearls were indeed thrown before swine. But I was not the one who did the throwing.

Have your pearls been snatched away? What Satan tells you is gone forever, God wants to restore. God wants to give you your pearls back, but I have found this gift is like "taking" them back. It is an active process, as God has empowered you to get back what has been stolen. Your pearls may have been taken by swine, but you can take them back!

Take Back Your Pearls talks about a beautiful exchange. God is waiting to give you the smooth, shiny gift of a restored soul, and all He asks in return is for the garbage you have been handed.

Patiently and lovingly, God waits to give us "beauty for ashes." This book will show you how to give up to God the negative issues that were dumped unwillingly on you, and then how to hold out your hand to Him in expectancy for the blessings that are already yours. Get ready to *Take Back Your Pearls.*

A Note

My abuser was a male. Statistically, the vast majority of sexual abusers are male. However, I do realize that females can be abusers too, and survivors of their actions are just as much in need of help. I believe the wisdom imparted to me by God and expressed in this book is relevant for all survivors, regardless of the gender of their abuser. However, for ease of reading, I have referred to the abuser with masculine pronouns throughout this book. Please know that I am not discrediting survivors of female abusers. I am simply trying to avoid the difficulty of reading that results from having to use two pronouns (him/her, his/hers, he/she) in every instance.

Chapter 1 — Triumph Over Tragedy

I had a very bad childhood. I might go as far as to say, I did not have a childhood at all—that I was robbed of one. The ugly, dark cloud of sexual abuse from my father dominated my growing up years.

There were good parts of my life. Thankfully, it was not just endless pain. But as many of you know, having that constant, scary ugliness threatening you every day, never knowing when it is going to strike again, has a way of coloring the whole thing black.

I know what it's like to suffer.

But more importantly, I know what it's like to heal. I feel like I have been led by God to share my journey, with the goal of helping others. All of our situations will be slightly different. All of our varying personalities will have responded to it differently. But there are some truths that apply to everyone.

1. You CAN heal. It is absolutely possible. It is not just a dream and it is not just for others. You do not have to stay in the pit that your past has put you in.

2. God WANTS you to heal. He has a future for you that is better than your past.

3. It is rarely an instant, miracle cure. It is a journey of hard work and determination. The healing is SO WORTH IT.

We are going to keep these truths in mind as we learn exactly how to heal.

I can remember as far back as being two years old, even as a toddler, my father sexually abused me. It would happen whenever we were alone together. He would climb into my bed with me at night to "tuck me in." There in the dark, he did hateful things. I knew I could not cry out to my mother. She knew where he was, so she must have known what he was doing.

He believed in corporal punishment as well, and I was spanked with a belt so hard it was difficult to sit down for days afterward while the welts and bruises were healing. From my earliest memories of life, I was terrified of my father. I was so scared to be alone with him that I would start shaking whenever we were.

My brother and sister endured the same horrors. In fact, they had it worse. We all prayed that someone would rescue us, that something would happen to take our father away. We even prayed that he would die. Such are the thoughts of panicked and abused little children.

It took years to realize the far-reaching extent of the abuse I endured. I was relieved to leave home after high school, to physically leave it behind me. Little did I know, I still carried it with me. The shame, the self-loathing, the fear of sexual intimacy in marriage—those were the things I knew about and prayed for healing for.

The things I did not know to pray about were my ingrained defaults. I was a doormat for the world, I had no backbone—

I was a chameleon who gave every audience what I thought it wanted. I had learned that my will meant nothing. I had learned to keep quiet and endure. I had learned that problems were solved by burying them and ignoring them, and then putting on a brave face.

I had been taught to live a lie. I learned how to build a perfect façade and then hide behind it, no matter how much I was crumbling and shrinking inside. God had a lot of work to do to make me into a productive adult.

I don't want to concentrate on the details of my abuse. I just want to lay the foundation by sharing some of what I endured to show the powerful and beautiful extent of the healing God did.

I want to start by saying that your pain is valid. Just because I will keep telling you that you can get over it does not mean I don't understand how awful and powerful it is. Also, your pain is uniquely yours, and is substantial no matter how many people have it worse.

I used to hear parents tell their children to eat their food because there were starving children in Africa. Did that really change how the children saw their food? Did it ever make them more hungry? *Someone else's reality will never be stronger than your reality.*

It is true that sometimes perspective can help us see our own situations differently. That is why I am willing to share my own experiences—to encourage you, comfort you, and let you know you are not alone. But my saying that your pain can be overcome does not invalidate it or take away from it.

I will spend most of this book exploring ways to heal and demonstrating how to put it all behind you. But that does not diminish the immensity of your hurt. I promise that I know the size of the mountains you are trying to move. In saying that they are movable, I am not taking away the truth of their enormity.

You have every right to feel the pain you are feeling. The myriad of emotions that cover the whole gamut have likely been flung at you and you have found yourself reeling. God knows that. He made you human and He does not hold it against you that you are hurting.

Please know that there is no lack of sympathy in my words. I will state upfront that what you have to go through to heal is completely unfair. Your abuser seems to get off scot-free while you are left with a painful journey just to get back to being normal. All of the things I am going to tell you to do, you should not have to do. I realize that. But the alternative is a lifetime of continued pain and suffering.

It is not fair. But it is worth it.

I am going to be dealing with what the Bible calls "the meat of the Word." On the other end of the spectrum is "the milk of the Word," what we need as babies in Christ. I am giving you the tough stuff. A baby is not able to chew meat, just as an adult cannot be sustained by milk. We are going to go all the way to complete victory, and that means tackling some hard issues. But your abuse was hard too.

Tough, deep-seated problems require tough, deep-reaching solutions. Perhaps you have tried other things. Perhaps you have tried everything the world has to offer, and you are still bearing the heavy yoke of pain. If you are ready for something that actually works, keep reading. This is not a Band-Aid fix, this is not topical cream—this is emotional and spiritual surgery. This will pluck out your pain, heal the area where it once resided, and leave you a whole and healthy person with a fantastic future ahead of you.

This may seem rather simplistic, but it is foundational: you must believe God's Word is true. The Bible is our instruction book for life. So many people are going through it without reading the directions. The best life we can possibly have is one that lines up with God's way of doing it. After all, He created us. He knows how we are supposed to function.

Make up your mind now to believe every word put forth in the Bible. If you dismiss something as outdated, not politically correct, or too difficult, you will miss out on your victory. I will show you how to take God's truths and put them to work in your life, today, right now, with as much power as they had when He wrote them. I will give you modern action words, things you can actually do that make sense in today's world. But you must first believe in the truth of God's instructions. And then you must take it one step further and believe that you CAN heal.

Know that God never instructs you to do something you cannot do. He tells us to be joyful despite our circumstances, forgive even those who are unforgivable, and do the right thing even when we have not gotten the right result. We can know with absolute certainty that those tough things are possible. God's Word says we can—so we CAN.

Lord, thank you that you want to heal me. Thank you that your plan for me does not include me staying in bondage to my painful past. I commit to this journey of healing. I know it will be hard and I ask you to strengthen me. Give me the will to seek my healing. Help me believe in the truth and power of your Word. Walk with me through this journey, hold my hand every step of the way, and help me to stay the course. In Jesus' name, amen.

Chapter 2 — Miracle or Journey?

Why can't I just get a miracle cure?

I did not deserve this in the first place, so why can't God heal me instantly?

God still knows how to do miracles. But He is more concerned with our spiritual and emotional maturity and our foundational healthiness than He is with our immediate comfort. God wants to *teach* us how to be victorious, not just *give* us an instant victory.

We would do the same thing with our own children. We enjoy giving them things, and we do it often. So does God. But in the years we are raising our children, we have to prepare them to be independent adults. They cannot have everything handed to them—they must learn how to do things for themselves. You give them money, but you teach them to have a good work ethic and how to earn their own money. You give them food, but you teach them how to cook so they can feed themselves.

God could take you out of something or God could take you through it. My experience is that most of the time, He takes us through it. If we trust Him, we must accept that this is better for us in the long run. Look at Joshua and the Battle of Jericho, and then look at Samson killing thousands with the donkey jawbone. In Joshua's case, they didn't even have to fight and the walls came tumbling down. God literally did that work for them. With Samson, he had to fight with his own hands to the point of exhaustion, but God still granted him victory.

Do not hold it against God if you did not get a Jericho. What if, instead, He is putting a donkey jawbone in your hand and giving you the power to fight against incredible odds?

God often sees more value in us going through a trial than having the trial instantly vanish. He wants us to have a victorious, overcoming *lifestyle*. That means our thoughts, actions, defaults, and mindsets have to line up with His truth. That comes through training, not through receiving a gift.

Yes, it is hard.

God never said it would be easy, and I will not say it either. If you thought that, then the first time it got tough, you would be shocked and hurt all over again, and you would likely abandon your quest. *So I do not mean to scare you, I mean to equip you.* Knowing it is hard means the hardness will not derail you.

If you know you are about to walk through some rough terrain, you put on hiking boots and take a bottle of water with you. You are prepared. Then the rocky trail and the steep hills don't surprise you and make you turn back. But if you thought it was a flat paved path and you set out in your flip flops, you would face hardship and disillusionment.

Make sure you differentiate between hard and too hard. That is vital. There is a Grand Canyon of difference between them. One is possible; one is impossible. God never asks us to do something we cannot do. But He does ask us to do hard things. When Satan whispers in your ear that it's hard, you tell him you know that, *but it's not too hard.*

Most things in life that are valuable are worth working for. Most of the important things don't just drop into our lap. God does this for a reason. It is in our human nature—the nature He made—to put more value in something we had to invest ourselves in—our time, our effort, our hearts, our money, our possessions. We can know that something is strong and firm when we've spent the time and effort to build it. Knowing this, don't despair that your healing journey isn't an instant miracle. Remember, it took years to get you to this point. Be willing to invest time into the coming back.

One sit-up doesn't give you hard abs. You would never expect it to. It will take many. But once you have that flat stomach, think of how much it means to you. Anybody who sees it knows you did not just do one sit-up. It took work, and the reward is something you can be very proud of.

Think of how much we admire people who have accomplished big things. Do we ever look at them and wish we could be like them? Then think of what they have done to get to that point. Olympic athletes didn't just walk up and get a medal. Their moment on the podium with that gold circle around their neck came after years of giving up other things to pursue a single-minded goal.

The star quarterback did not just walk onto the field and take the glory. Preparing for that moment took hours of sweat and pain, hours of sometimes frustrating, "unglorious" parts. We enjoy the piano virtuoso with the spotlight on him in his tuxedo as he plays the big, shiny grand piano on a stage. But how many hours, that turned into months and years, did he practice?

There are many examples around us of people who achieved a worthy goal by trying hard. Everybody's journey is different, but remember these "heroes" when the going gets tough. Remember how beautiful and amazing the goal you are working toward is. Know that victory over a painful past, that ushers in a future full of hope and success, is more precious than any medal or trophy.

The biggest resistance I have encountered so far when talking to other victims is their sense of injustice. What happened to them is completely unfair. The strength and magnitude of this feeling is so great, it overrides everything. They are right in-part—it IS unfair. Tragically so. But they are letting that injustice keep them from acting. They should not have to fix a problem they did not create. Especially a huge one that will take so much effort on their part, and none on the part of the abuser. They shouldn't have to, and so they don't.

I encourage you to brace yourself for the unfairness to hit you. It will. Prepare yourself now to accept it. It's one thing to determine to work hard to earn an Olympic medal. It's another thing to determine to work hard to fix a huge, painful mess someone else created. It's not just hard work, it's unfair, hard work. That is the harsh truth that makes up the foundation on which you will be building. If you cannot build on that foundation, you will not see your victory.

Imagine you were in a car accident, hit by a drunk driver. You ended up in the hospital in critical condition. You were thankful to be alive, but you faced a long, hard journey to heal your body. How do you feel when your stitches are removed, your bruising is gone, your casts have come off, and you are told it is now time for physical therapy?

Up to that point, all you had to do was survive. You just had to lay there and let your body heal. But now, you face a very painful journey. Hours of physical therapy will test your limits, make you sweat, make you cry, and make you shake with effort and exhaustion. Do you refuse to do it because it's not your fault and it's unfair that your body is broken? Chances are you overlook that part. You probably go through with it, knowing that a whole and healthy body in the end is worth it, even though a drunk driver put you there, even though the drunk driver doesn't have to do a single minute of physical therapy.

We must look at our emotional health the same way. We must not shy away from the intense therapy it will require. We must look at the goal, not the reasons why we are here. We do not want to stay here. Regardless of the past, we must determine to make a change for the future.

The bottom line is YOU are the only one who can fix YOU. Facing this tough journey requires embracing this idea: It is not my fault, but I am my only solution.

One other faulty mindset I want to address besides, "Why can't I get an instant miracle cure?" is, "Why can't I just let time heal me?"

The short answer is simply this: the cliché is not true. Time does not heal all wounds. The world says that, and at the beginning of my journey, I believed it. I have lost loved ones and I felt how the intense grief of those first weeks thankfully did not last forever. But time is not a miracle "cure for all." A huge wound like abuse does not just go away with time. You have probably lived long enough to see that. *You have to MAKE it go away.* Leaving that precious solution to time is essentially saying you are not going to DO anything. You are just going to hunker down and hope. How far has that gotten you?

A wound like abuse becomes an abscess. I used to work at a veterinary clinic and I would see wounds, particularly on cats, that abscessed under the skin. It did not look like much on the outside, but there was a large pocket of pus under the skin, growing and spreading and infecting nearby tissues. If left untreated, it would kill the cat. Time would not heal it; optimistically looking at the surface and declaring that all looked fine would not make it go away. The only solution was to find it, completely drain it, and then stitch up the opening. We need to do that too. We cannot rely on time—we need to do it ourselves—do it deliberately, do it completely.

I cannot stress enough that it is worth it. I don't want my examples of tough training journeys and unfair reasons to intimidate you. I want you to be prepared, so that Satan cannot derail you when the terrain gets rocky. I want you to throw aside any "bumper sticker" excuses the world may give you for not taking action. But now that we've talked about it being hard and unfair, we need to stress over and over again how much it's worth it. The reward so far outweighs the work, that it would never fit into an equal equation.

Lord, thank you that you love me enough to teach me a new lifestyle. Thank you that you know better than me what I need. I ask that you help me progress through my healing journey as quickly as possible, but I will not get discouraged when it doesn't happen overnight. Help me to keep my eyes on the goal of complete healing. Help me not get discouraged when the journey is hard and unfair. I accept that, and I choose to proceed despite it. In Jesus' name, amen.

Chapter 3 — Define Yourself

The first step on a healing journey is to take a look at the most important part—you. We will deal later with finding happiness, controlling negative thoughts, learning forgiveness, etc. But right now I want you to examine the platform you will be using to do all that. Let's look at you. How do you view yourself?

Everything you will eventually be doing comes from you. That may be stating the obvious. But you may not yet know the real foundation you are working from: your automatic mindsets, your defaults, and how they have been changed by your abuse. Making sure that your foundation is solid is the place you have to start. You would not add beautiful furniture to a house that was crumbling. You will not work towards your future, or even accept that you have a good one, if you think you are a used-up, unworthy, defiled mess.

You have to know that you are OK. Then you have to take one step further—you have to like yourself. And then you have to take one final step—you have to love yourself. This glorious accomplishment is entirely possible. But to get there, you must define yourself properly. That means accepting the truth of who you are, and rejecting the lies about who you are.

That is often difficult. Satan whispers foulness and hatred in our ears and we accept it because we have been trodden down so much that it is just easier. Our past is a mess, our desires have been squelched, our futures look dim—how can we be OK?

Well, because God says we are.

Right now, with all our messiness, all our failure, all our disappointment and pain, God loves us with a perfect love. God says we are valuable. God says we are worthy. God says we are deserving of happiness. It is amazing what God can look past.

I will explain this in a way that eventually made sense to me when I looked back. When you have been abused, you want to throw out anything tainted by your abuser—things he gave you, things that remind you of him, things that look or smell like him. That is good and fine and healthy.

But what if YOU are the tainted thing?

What happens when you cannot throw yourself away? You must see yourself and love yourself the way God does. You will never undo the tainting of the past by wishing it wasn't so. But by simply believing that God's Word is true, you will find incredible freedom. You will see yourself as worthy, especially worthy of saving. You are the righteousness of God. God cloaking you in righteousness the moment you accepted salvation is infinitely stronger than another human being tainting you with ugliness.

Self-hate is not holy. God does not want us to harbor it. God wants us to love ourselves. Not in an arrogant way, but in a way that reflects the love He has for us. We can hate what happened to us, or hate the defaults it has caused in our behavior. But we must turn from any hate of WHO we are and exchange that for love.

Think of a self-deprecating person and how annoying it is to listen to them. When you try to compliment someone and they just turn it around and say how horrible they are, how does that make you feel? When someone who is slim and beautiful complains how fat and ugly they are, how does that make you feel? When people talk down about themselves and refuse to see any of the talent shining from them, God is hurt. God has given every one of us beautiful things on the inside, and He wants us to acknowledge them and enjoy them.

I realize you are not going to go from feeling so down about yourself to suddenly thinking you are amazing. But that is the goal, and I want to start you on your journey. I want you to begin to see how amazing you actually are. When you realize how great a person has been violated, it will help you throw off all the garbage your abuser heaped onto you.

God does not say a single negative thing about you in the Bible. Not one. But He says plenty of positive things. You may think right away that people got rebuked, and that is correct. But it was behavior that was being corrected, not people's identity being put down. God looks at WHO we are and what we DO as separate things. No matter what you do, *and no matter what someone else does to you,* those beautiful things God says about who you are are still true.

Just to give you a glimpse, if you are a believer, God says in His Word that you are: anointed, able, blessed, complete, confident, consecrated, chosen, bold, loved, accepted, dedicated, disciplined, wise, discerning, obedient, humble, patient, favored, equipped, talented, strong, faithful, fearless, peaceful, joyful, free, kind, gentle, gracious, guiltless, redeemed, justified, sanctified. And there are many more. All these things describe you!

Here is where you must ask yourself, "Who is stronger, my abuser or my God?" It is easy to say that God is stronger. *But you must come to the point that you accept it in your heart.* When you look in the mirror, you need to see a child of God, not a used and discarded product of another person.

Let God define you.

God has already done a perfect job of this. But we need to accept it. We have accepted salvation that we did not deserve. We can gratefully take the gift He handed us, and let it change our lives forever. With the same mindset, we need to believe it when God says He sees us as righteous through the shed blood of His Son. This is not about forgiveness, repentance, striving, or earning. This is about you, just as you are, right now, with your entire past hanging all over you—you are the righteousness of God.

God will help you at any moment, just like a parent would help a child who suddenly called out, "Mom, help!" God will never love you more than He loves you right now. His love is perfect, unbound by mistakes, and not subject to whims or moods or preferences. When you are completely healed, He will not love you more. He already loves you with His whole heart.

Grab onto that truth and never let go. You ARE the righteousness of God. He sees you through the shed blood of Jesus and He will never change His mind on that. Your abuser has absolutely NO power to take away your righteousness. It was given by God and He will never take it away. Claim that. Believe that!

This is the first time I will say this, but you will recognize it as a common theme. You need to declare your truth out loud. Say the words. The Bible tells us there is power in the tongue. Spoken words created the world, spoken words can build someone up or tear them down. God speaks much in His Word about what we say because He knows how powerful it is. He even calls our tongue a weapon. Well, good—let's use it as a weapon to defeat the enemy.

Say out loud, "God is stronger than my abuser." Say out loud, "I am righteous, worthy, and lovable." Declare these things anytime you think of it, while looking in the mirror, in the morning when your day begins, and at night when your day ends.

The words you say can be different for everybody. I encourage you to identify where you have been attacked the most. What is keeping you from believing you are righteous through Christ? If you could have God tell you one beautiful thing about yourself, what would it be?

Some of the truths I have declared out loud over the years are, "God loves me right now", "I am not tainted," and, "God thinks I am beautiful." Find the truth that resonates with you and speak it into your soul.

The Bible says we defeat Satan with the word of our testimony. When you know that your words are weapons, aim them at the enemy and fire away. When you can't say them out loud, turn them into prayer. Ask God to help you grasp the truth of those amazing promises.

Here is another statement you need to fully grasp: You have authority over your life. That is your right as a believer. It is part of your inheritance, and you did not have to earn it. The decision to overcome your past is your right. It might be hard to do, but the *authority* to do it is yours. The Bible says that God has given us "authority over all the power the enemy possesses." Satan has no authority in your life! He knows that, but he does not want you to know it.

You may not feel like that final authority is yours. You have been abused and trampled, knocked down and disregarded. If you are like I was, you feel like you don't have one shred of authority over your own life. But God says you do. So why doesn't it feel like it? Because Satan has power. And he does everything he can to wield that power to your harm. You need to understand the difference between power and authority. Authority is stronger, it is the highest, it is final. Power is influence. That is what Satan has.

You will never stand up and use your authority if you do not know you have it. So believe God's Word. He has given you rights just like your country's constitution has given you rights. You would not let someone take away your rights as an American citizen, then do not let Satan take away your rights as a child of God.

I like using analogies and putting God's Word into today's world. So here is an example to illustrate my point. If you said something on the street about who God is and a policeman came over and tried to handcuff you and arrest you and accused you of breaking the law by saying that, how would you react? You would come back with what you KNOW to be true, and that is that you have the right to say what you want. You are guaranteed freedom of speech by the constitution of this country. Knowing that, you can stand up to someone like a policeman, who has more power than you, and deny his charge against you.

Similarly, you need to know your rights in Christ. Then you can use them to stand up against Satan's power and accusations. You have a right to peace, joy and victory. You have the authority over Satan's manipulations to gain those wonderful things. He can influence you with his power, but you can put him right back in his place with your authority. Know who you are in Christ. And know your rights as a child of God.

Another important aspect of examining YOU is taking a look at how you identify yourself. We all have multiple aspects that make up who we are. If someone asked you, "Who are you?", how would you respond? You may say that you are a Christian, a wife, a mother, a teacher, an accountant, a violin player, a basketball player, etc. We define ourselves mostly by our family roles, our occupation, our hobbies, and our faith. What you may not realize is that you wear another identity marker: victim.

You probably wouldn't name "victim" as part of your identity if someone asked you, but look inside. How much of who you are comes from that? Do you hate men? Do you struggle to have a fulfilling sex life? Do you constantly seek control over others? Do you give up control instantly and let the world walk all over you? Do you have bitterness and resentment that ooze into other aspects of your life?

This was brought home to me more when watching my sister than in looking inside myself. It was seeing her that made me ask God these hard questions about myself. She was always blaming her past abuse for her current actions. It was the reason she could act promiscuously. It was the reason she could drink excessively. It was the reason she could fight selfishly with her husband. She even verbalized on numerous occasions, "I'm a victim." What she didn't verbalize, but what she did live, was, "Therefore, I can …"

Her being a victim became a huge part of her identity. But she did not see it that way. That led me to get on my knees before God and humble myself to ask if I was doing that too. How much of your identity would you give to "victim" right now? Is it bigger than being a wife or mother or daughter or sister? Is it bigger than being a Christian?

Now ask yourself, what would others say in answer to that same question? They get to observe your words and actions. They are the receivers of what you put out. Would they draw the same conclusion as you? Lastly, think about how God would answer that question. He who knows all truth and sees through all personal defenses and excuses, He knows exactly how much being a victim is defining you. Chances are God puts the victim percentage of your identity higher than you do. Chances are you are not even aware of how much your past is defining you.

Whether you think the world owes you leniency or different rules because you were abused, or whether you do not even realize how much your past is defining you, you can still be set free in the same way. We are going to take "victim" out of the description of you. Your past cannot be erased, but it will go from being something that controls and defines you to something that happened to you.

You need to realize that you have an identity, and then determine that you will be in charge of it. Your abuser hurt you, but he does not get to define you. You do. Your past happened, irrefutably, but it does not get to define you. You do. You get to decide if your pain or your past *becomes* you.

The first step in taking control and banishing your "victim" title is to accept, fully, where you are right now. And take responsibility for it. The cry of your heart at this moment is probably, "But I'm NOT responsible!" Look at it this way. You are not responsible for having gotten to this point, but you are responsible for where you go from here. It is not your fault that you ended up here, but it is your responsibility to take a different direction. Your abuse is the reason you are here, but do not let it become the excuse to stay here.

Whichever wording resonates with you, embrace it. Tell yourself, "From this moment on, I am in charge. With God's help, I make all the decisions. My abuser and my past do not get to decide any details about my life anymore." Taking responsibility for where you are does not mean you are blaming yourself. It means you are recognizing that you are the one who has to change it.

Just think—the alternative is to ask your abuser to do his proper responsibility and fix you. That won't happen! The only one who can make the change is you. Therefore, you are responsible. Even if you feel like you are in the deepest, darkest, smelliest, ugliest pit, tell yourself, "Okay, I'm in a horrible pit. So be it. This is where I'm starting. I'm in charge, and I'm going to get out."

One visual that helped me was to see myself as a chunk of clay. I felt like a flat, shapeless, ugly chunk. But I realized I had a choice. I could go through life like that, continually saying it's unfair and painful to be flat, shapeless and ugly. Or I could put in some effort to reshape myself.

I saw too many people going through life dragging their current shape, wanting pity and understanding from the world, and constantly seeing the ugliness in the mirror. I thought of years going by and me still being my same shape. I did not want that. I don't know what beautiful final result God has in mind for me, but it starts with gentle prodding and rubbing to reshape the clay. Even one little indentation in that clay means change. And that means progress, something different in the mirror.

If I defend my right to stay the same, to get pity from the world, to claim I should not have to reshape my entire being, then I'll get what I'm crying for—sameness. I'll be flat and shapeless and ugly forever. I will have saved myself the pain of change. But how painful is it to stay the same?

Knowing your foundation helps you do battle. Look inside, ask God for revelation, and try to discern where "victim" has defined you. It may simply be a matter of accepting that it has, without knowing the details. It may be overwhelming to see and accept that many of your behaviors stem from your victim mentality. Either way, do not worry. We will deal with behaviors later. For now, we are just going to be truthful about taking a good deep look at ourselves, and then taking responsibility for everything, right now, so that we can proceed to change it.

Lord, thank you that you love me with a perfect love. Thank you that your love does not depend on actions done by me or to me. Thank you that I have righteousness through you just by believing, and that righteousness is mine forever—nobody can take it away. Thank you that I have authority through you that is stronger than Satan's power. Help me to see myself the way you see me. Help me to love myself and believe that I am worthy. Lord, I accept your definition of me, not my abuser's. I do not want to be a victim anymore. Help me to face the ways my past may be defining me, so that I can take control and create my own definition in You. Help me take responsibility for myself entirely, so that I can change. In Jesus' name, amen.

Chapter 4—Guilt Is Not Noble

OK, so you learned that you have to love yourself and shed your victim mentality. How do you do that when you feel like a wretched, used-up mess? As we learned in the last chapter, you have to believe God's Word when He says you are the righteousness of the Lord. You have to know that you have Godly authority over your life, and embrace that truth. You also need to take an honest look inside and take responsibility for where you are in order to move forward.

Let's look a little deeper.

It's hard to love yourself when you're filled with guilt and condemnation. Your abuser dumped those on you. If you feel them, it's not your fault. Unfortunately, it's your responsibility to get rid of them. The good news is, you will feel so wonderful when you do.

I have noticed that some people carry guilt around like it's noble, like they are a martyr. I don't know why it's easier for us to embrace the negative than it is the positive. But that seems to be human nature. Just in case you are thinking that at least you are being humble and somehow good by berating yourself, let me state again that guilt is not noble.

Guilt is from Satan. Conviction is from God. They are so different. Conviction is the loving reprimand that tells us we are headed in the wrong direction. It guides us to the right direction. Conviction leads to repentance. Conviction has a noble goal of helping us. Guilt simply says we are bad. And leaves us there.

If it's any comfort, I can tell you I walked that heavy path for years. I hated the arrogance that I saw in people, especially people like my father. To take what you want when it hurts others so badly was pure cockiness in my mind. Perhaps as a reaction to that, I valued humility. That is all well and good. But I saw humbleness as hanging my head and bearing guilt and dragging myself through a suboptimal life. That is not Godly humility. Humility does not dictate that you must be the world's doormat.

I stated in the last chapter that you must accept responsibility for where you're at. That does not mean accepting guilt. Please understand how different these are. Guilt is a tool of Satan that he will use to beat you down constantly. And it is so foundationally versatile for him! He can keep you from any number of victories by instead turning your attention to guilt.

So many abuse victims buy into the lie that it was somehow their fault. As an adult, I looked back and wondered with shame why I never cried out for help. Why didn't I go to an aunt or uncle or other family member? Why didn't I say something to a teacher or counsellor at school? Why didn't I run up to the nearest policeman? These things never even entered my head as a child. Fear ruled my thoughts. I was told not to tell, so I didn't tell. I was alone and trapped. There was no way out.

I did make one feeble attempt to cry out for help. Sadly, it only made me feel worse. When I was 10 years old, I went to my mother. With my stomach tied in knots and fear oozing out of me, I explained what Dad was doing to me. I told her how much I hated it. She sent me right back to him. I can't even put into words how I felt walking away from her that day on shaky little legs. I was completely alone, and sick with despair. There would never be any help. And even worse—the reason Mom wasn't helping me must be because I wasn't worthy of help. I wasn't important enough or loved enough to get her protection. I must be bad, and that only added to the guilt.

My only means of survival was to endure. It is this mindset that leads to foundational defaults being set and built on for years to come. And it is this mindset that can also lead to guilt. "I let it happen," "I did nothing to stop it," or the worst one that is so hard to be talked out of, "It happened. I ended up defiled, therefore I am guilty of being defiled."

That mindset reaches its tentacles everywhere, and starts controlling things on a subconscious level. People who buy into that lie will live a life in the shadows, not trying to reach as high as other "normal" people, content with the crumbs of life, lowering their standards, and taking whatever life hands them because they are "lesser" people. It can affect what jobs they take, what people they befriend, who they date, what hobbies they choose, where they choose to live, whether or not they take care of their health, and on and on. Guilt will keep a person down, chained to a lesser life.

You must let go of your guilt.

Guilt, shame, and condemnation can all be rolled into one. They come down to the same base feeling, with the same negative consequences. They must all be banished. There is shame inherent in sex being misused. But we must find the strength to lay the shame at our abuser's feet. And leave it there. Any other person would see the fault as entirely the abuser's, but somehow we pick it up along the way. Put it back where it belongs. You did not do this to yourself. You did not choose this. You did not want this. Every fiber of your being screamed against it. Use the strength of your abhorrence of it to place the blame where it belongs. Declare out loud that you will NOT take blame and bear guilt. Declare out loud that the shame is not yours.

Romans 8:1 says that there is no condemnation for those who believe. Can it be that simple? Can you dare to free yourself from a burden of condemnation just because God's Word says you can? Whenever Satan tries to attack you with guilt, quote scripture back to him. Over and over. Your abuser hurt you, but *he has no power to condemn you.*

Your abuser took what he wanted at the time, perhaps many times like my father did. He was not thinking of your future, or probably even his future. He was gratifying his basest desires at your expense. He was not thinking, *I am doing this to ruin your future. You WILL think of me anytime life tries to give you something good, and you will turn it down because of the shame I am shoving on you. This will haunt you forever, change your defaults, and make you a lesser person.* No, your abuser was not thinking that. He was simply thinking selfishly that you were a means to an end for him. You were usable at the moment.

But so many of us take up that mantle somewhere along the way. A deviant sexual act does not remain closed in the moment of time it happened. It leeches out into anything else it can reach. And we let it. It is human to do so. We understand why. But still, we must stop it. We must declare that it ends right now. We must relegate it back to being a horrible thing that happened to us, but not something that will keep happening to us. We must cut off its tentacles of influence.

So we stop guilt right in its tracks.

Though feelings of guilt may continue to pop up, use your knowledge of the truth of guilt to overcome them. Feelings are not facts. Feelings can be taken captive, and our thoughts should have control over them. When you feel guilty, say out loud that that feelings are not the truth. Declare that the truth is *you bear no guilt.* Declare that God does not condemn you and, therefore, you refuse to condemn yourself.

I said at the beginning of this chapter that guilt was not noble because that was my own personal journey. Looking back, I realize that somehow I thought it was. Some of you may identify guilt right away as the imposter that it is. Some may rise up against it and rage a lifelong battle with it. Unfortunately, I simply gave in to it. I was not a fighter. I had only been taught to accept and endure.

I can say now that letting guilt define me was the easy track. I would learn later that the harder track was to fight it and overcome it. But at the time, I did not even have the means to identify it. I didn't even see it for what it was. It led to me wrongly defining humility, which led to me being a doormat for the world. For years I felt stomped on. I had no backbone. I was simply reactionary.

If we continue to come back to our basic definition of ourselves as "the righteousness of God," it will help us to define everything that follows. If we are the righteousness of God, then we should not be a doormat for anyone. If God wants us to have humility, it is a healthy humility. It is a mindset that allows us to serve our God and our fellow human beings, not getting puffed up with arrogance, but knowing that we are uniquely made and we have something unique to offer the world.

Similarly, let's consider our righteousness in God as we consider what conviction should feel like. We know that guilt and condemnation are never from God, but that does not mean He will never correct us. Learning to distinguish between conviction and condemnation will help us put the devil in his place. Conviction is always loving. It always guides us in the right direction. It always prompts us for positive change. It always lines up with God's word. If we feel guilt and God's Word says we don't need to, then we know it's not conviction. And we change our mindset and declare the truth instead.

Lord, I come to you with my guilt, and I declare that I will bear it no more. Thank you for your Word that tells me I am not condemned. Thank you for the truth that though my abuse was horrible, it was not my fault. Please let the truth and freedom that you offer be stronger than my guilty feelings. Help me to learn the difference between condemnation and conviction. Help me to declare your truth over and over, every time guilt tries to creep in. Thank you for setting me free. Please help me to love myself even more as I let go of my guilt forever. In Jesus' name, amen.

LORIE KAY

Chapter 5—Forgiveness

You now have a good foundation of knowing who you are in Christ and why you are valuable and lovable, and you have recognized some of Satan's most powerful tools—guilt and condemnation. Now you are going to move on to another big step in your journey to secure freedom from your past.

You need to forgive your abuser.

This is a really tough one. I struggled with this for years. Remember how I told you at the beginning of this book that you MUST believe God's Word is true? Here is where it gets serious. God's Word tells us to forgive, and it further explains that it is for our own good. In a human way, that just doesn't make sense. If you are going to progress, you must set aside your human feelings, and believe, believe, believe that God's Word is true.

It would have been so much easier if God had told us to forgive the little things. He might have shown some sympathy and mercy by letting us off the hook for really big, horrible, damaging things. Surely, He understands that we cannot forgive those?

But no. God does not put ANY restrictions or limits on who or what to forgive. We are to forgive everybody, for everything, every time.

The dictionary tells us that forgiving is "to give up resentment," "to exact neither punishment nor redress," "to stop feeling anger," "to pardon an offender." I came across a definition that was credited to psychologists, that stated "forgiveness is a conscious, deliberate decision to release feelings of resentment or vengeance toward a person or group who has harmed you." All of these definitions give us good action words, but notice the action is all on us, the forgiver. Nothing is mentioned of any obligation of the offender. It is not pending an apology or a request, or anything done by the offender to put in motion this release you are to give them.

Forgiveness automatically means there is harm, there is damage, there is punishment deserved, there is an offense, there is anger—all of that is assumed where forgiveness is needed. So we must not ever let the presence of those things dictate that we cannot forgive. The presence of all that negativity is the very reason why forgiveness is needed in the first place.

Forgiveness is huge. It is a decision you will have to make again and again. Forgiveness is a choice. It is something you purposely do, in obedience to God, subjecting your feelings to the overriding authority of the truth. It is not fair. It is not comfortable. But it IS effective. It DOES work.

I decided that I was going to forgive my father when the truth of God's Word had impressed itself strongly enough in my heart. I really wanted to do the right thing. So I prayed to God as a teenager, telling Him that I forgave Dad. I asked for God's help to do it and declared it done.

And then wondered why nothing changed.

For me, it was a journey of having to reclaim my victory over and over. My decision did not change, but circumstances made my feelings war with my will. Now that I am married, I can see that forgiveness is like love. Both are decisions. Both are commitments. Both need to be upheld in the absence of feelings. Both need to be nurtured and declared, many times.

As I mentioned earlier, our words are weapons that we can use in our fight, and we must state our truths out loud as much as possible. I have said, "I forgive my father," countless times. When negative feelings rear their ugly heads, I say my truth to knock them back down. When my father does something else to hurt me and it feels like it is stacked on top of all those other years of hurt, I say my truth.

I am sure this will manifest itself in different ways for each of you. Perhaps just that moment of finally telling God you are willing to forgive and declaring it for the first time will flood you with release. Perhaps you won't have to fight for your victory like I did, nor wonder why the feeling got robbed, and why you needed to "go through it all over again."

I think it was particularly tough for me because I was living with my abuser. I couldn't get away from him. On the surface, we had a father-daughter relationship that was expected to be upheld. I was not allowed to kick him out of my life and just get rid of him once and for all. When I left home, our relationship changed, but it was still there. Phone calls and visits happened, milestones of life happened and were shared with him. I had to constantly face him. So Satan had many chances to try to undo my decision to forgive.

Had it been one isolated instance and I never again had to look into my abuser's eyes, it would have been easier to forgive. Or so I told myself. Everybody's journey is different. I was a Christian, and wanted to love my father. The Bible told me I had to honor him anyway, so he was already involved in my obedience to God, regardless of whether he was a good or bad father. At least I got to see my father doing good things, showing the good side of his character. Other victims whose abusers were strangers will only ever see a mask of cruelty in their minds when they remember them. Does having a relationship with your abuser make it harder or easier to forgive? I do not know. I thought for years that it was harder for me because of my personality, but I stopped trying to figure it out. God says to forgive. Period. We are all tasked with that instruction. So our energies are best spent getting on with it.

Forgiveness does NOT mean condoning your abuser's behavior. Do not ever make the mistake of equating forgiveness with acceptance. Forgiving him does not mean you suddenly think it's OK. It does not take away from the seriousness of the crime. It does not take away from your pain. In no way does forgiving diminish the experience. I initially thought that forgiving meant I automatically felt OK about the whole thing. And, therefore, I could not forgive until I did. That is not true. It comes down to this: *forgiving has nothing to do with feelings.*

If you wait until you feel like it, you never will. At no point in your life, even after you have claimed full victory and your past has no power to hurt or control you, will you ever state that you felt like forgiving because the negativity disappeared. You must forgive BECAUSE there is negativity. You must do it knowing you will not feel like it.

Painful things done to us, especially ones of the magnitude of abuse, automatically cause a "debt" feeling. We were wronged, so we are owed something from the perpetrator. Our society understands this fully, and manifests it in our justice system. Criminals are arrested, tried in court, and punished for their wrongdoing. Witnesses are able to explain how the criminal hurt them, and a punishment suitable to the crime is laid upon the criminal. It does not make up for murder, theft, violence, and destruction, but it does address the idea of a debt being owed. To the best of the ability of the judicial powers of society, criminals pay the debt they incurred by prison time, monetary fines, community service, etc.

We feel that debt too. Our abusers owe us something. But the toughest part of this equation of debt is that they simply cannot pay. They cannot give us anything to make up for what they took from us. My father owes me a childhood. Rapists may owe victims their innocence back. How can an abuser ever pay the debt of a physically broken body, a disease, a suicide attempt, years of therapy, an abortion, or an unwanted child? If withholding forgiveness could cause them to pay their debt, then that would not only be the system God ordained, but the system every society would embrace as well.

We all know it does not work that way.

Not even watching your abuser get thrown into prison will satisfy the debt he owes you. And considering the shameful and repulsive nature of these crimes, very few victims have the stomach to get through the judiciary process enough to end that way. Identifying your abuse as a debt and acknowledging that it can never be repaid allows you to better see forgiveness as a solution. It is literally the only way to set yourself free from the debt mindset that the abuse placed over you. You can tear up that I.O.U.

Forgiveness comes back to that original sense of injustice that I talked about at the beginning: it is so unfair. You should not have to forgive. You should not have to tackle this big mountain of feelings, and beat it down with the truth like you're having a battle with it. But you must. Pray for the grace to accept the unfairness of it as you travel your forgiveness journey. And if it's a battle, then determine you're going to win. If you have to keep using truth to beat down feelings, know that eventually they will be fully beaten, and you will have won. Truth is a mighty weapon. You cannot use it repeatedly without getting results.

One thing that helped me with the idea of forgiveness, and particularly the injustice of it, was to understand that God first forgave me. It is summed up in the Bible in short, succinct statements, but the power within them is immense. God does it to us first, so we can experience the receiving end of it, and then He instructs us to be like Him, and do it for others. *He does not expect us to give what we have not first received.*

Think about that. If God wanted you to pay a debt and you said, "But Lord, I have no money," and so God gave you the money, you would simply be giving to your creditor what was given to you. That is a very simple illustration, but it helped me to think of it like that. I would rather keep the money, but God gave it to me in the first place, and then He told me to give it away. If you think you don't have it to give, believe God's Word and know that you do. He gave it to you. He would never expect you to do something impossible. So you can. And He will help you.

You probably think you are a good person. I did. So we can't possibly be needing the same kind of forgiveness that our abusers do, right? Wrong. God was kind and gentle about bringing this truth fully into my heart, so I want to be kind and gentle about telling you too. I don't want to put you down, or make you feel bad about yourself. I want you to see the incredible beauty of what God has done for you in forgiving you. *You need forgiveness just as much as your abuser does.* That is a hard statement to accept. But remember that God does not weigh sin. We do. To God, all sin is equal in its wrongness.

To us, it makes a difference if people were hurt, and how badly they were hurt. Punching a small child on the playground and stealing thousands of dollars from the government by tax evasion are completely different for us. But not for God. Lying to a friend to get out of a lunch you no longer want to do and lying on the witness stand under oath in a courtroom are completely different for us. But not for God. We are guilty of innumerable offenses. All of them are covered under the shed blood of Christ, but just think—God has to forgive us every day. Here is where true Godly humility comes in. When we can grasp how much God has had to forgive us for, then we can understand why He has the right to ask us to forgive others.

Jesus explains this to us in His parable in Matthew 18. The servant who owed his master millions of dollars could not pay and begged for mercy. He was given it. His debt was forgiven. Set free, the servant went outside and ran into someone who owed him several thousand dollars, a much lesser debt. This man couldn't pay either, but instead of showing the mercy that was just demonstrated to him, the servant had the man thrown in prison. When the master found out, he rebuked the servant for not showing mercy, and he was not only thrown into prison, he was also tortured.

This parable is to all of us. And it's not about money, it's about forgiveness. Every one of us has been cleared of our debt of millions, and is being asked to then clear others of their debt of thousands. You will never forgive anyone for more than God has forgiven you. You cannot out-forgive God. Whenever it hurts to forgive your abuser, remember that God has forgiven you. But give that the weight it deserves. God has forgiven you *for more than you are forgiving your abuser.* That will make you humble! I keep coming back to our absolute need to believe God's Word, because when we do, we see the tremendous magnitude of the truth. The Bible says the truth will set us free. And this is one instance where it does just that. Forgive with thanksgiving and humility, because God first forgave you.

One common thought that keeps people from forgiving is the notion that it somehow "socks it to the abuser" to withhold forgiveness. We somehow think justice is more served by staying angry at them, and "letting them off the hook" is too good for them. My response to that is this: They don't care one bit. It does not hurt them at all for you to stay angry and eaten up with unforgiveness. In many cases, your abuser will never see you again, and your mindset towards them has absolutely zero effect on them. Even if you do see them, maybe all the time, like in my situation, your mindset towards their abuse of you won't even enter their heads.

My abuse was a taboo topic in our household. It was never discussed, and I was supposed to continue to play the normal role of a daughter. My father had no idea if I had forgiven him or not. He never asked. Most abusers don't have any interest in finding out how you view them. Even while living every day right next to him for years, I never got to demonstrate to my father how I felt. When I left home and our relationship changed to one with a physical distance, I realized even more how forgiveness was all about *my* life, not his. He had no idea how much of my personality or actions or mindsets were because of him. He had no idea if I was or wasn't forgiving him, and how that may change how I interacted with him. The sad truth was, not only did he not know, he probably did not care.

That really brought home to me the truth of forgiveness: Don't think of it as something between you and your abuser. Think of it as something between you and God. Do it out of obedience to God. Do it to release yourself. Your anger, kept pent up and oozing bitterness into other areas of life, *does not ooze out onto your abuser.* It only robs your own peace and joy. I've heard it described many ways, but this one stuck with me—refusing to forgive is like drinking poison and expecting your enemy to die.

Unforgiveness is poison. Somebody put something bad into you, and you are insisting on keeping it there when you refuse to forgive. So it does what poison does—it festers and spreads and kills. Forgiveness releases it out of you, breaks its binds on you. There is no way to fight evil with evil. God says this in Romans and in Peter. You cannot fight negativity with more negativity, and win. The only way to gain victory is to overcome evil with good. You fight negativity with positivity. This manifests in many ways, but one of them is to forgive. Unforgiveness just fuels the fire. It keeps heaping negativity onto negativity. That won't fix anything.

All of this is to try to show you the reasons why you should forgive. At its basis is the "because I said so" reasoning: God told us to. If we were that spiritually mature, that is all we would need. But our soul cries out for explanation, for something to make sense. God's Word says forgiveness sets us free, but we want to know why and how. This is one chapter I suggest you read over and over. I feel like the importance of it requires me to say it in a million different ways, to cover pages and pages with it so it shines through in every possible way. I will just say, with all my heart, that *you must make the decision to forgive.*

God sees your heart and will see your intent the moment you decide it. I believe God rewards that. He doesn't enjoy setting up an obstacle course in front of us and seeing how thoroughly He can trip us up. He wants to help us. He doesn't give us an easy journey, but He gives us Himself as a constant help. Cry out to Him. As I've said before, start by declaring your decision. There is power in saying the truth. Say out loud, "I forgive my abuser." Fill in the name so it has more power. I said, "I forgive Dad for sexually abusing me for years." That stated the whole thing. And I've said it over and over. Every time you say it, you pound another nail in the coffin of unforgiveness.

What else can you do? I feel like wanting to forgive is a big step. Once I got there, and made a habit of stating my truth, I felt like there was more I should be doing. Forgiveness is a big thing. I didn't expect my feelings to line up right away, but I felt like there should be more action behind it. If you want to move onward and upward, God will always show you how!

There are three things you can actually DO to demonstrate and strengthen your forgiveness. Please know that these come after your initial decision to forgive. That desire to do God's will must come first, and that is what God recognizes. You can still try to do these things on the outside, but if you haven't made the decision to forgive on the inside, these won't work.

The first thing is to treat your abuser well. That sounds heinous, so let me explain. It comes from the premise of giving good treatment to people who don't first give it to you. The Bible states it in Matthew: "Love your enemies, bless them that curse you, do good to them that hate you." If a friend or coworker gossips about you, or stands you up for a meeting, or lies to you, you still have to interact with them. Treating them well will be something you can practice on a daily or weekly basis. In that context, this idea makes more sense—we can handle it on a smaller scale. But it also applies on a larger scale, to more hurtful situations. God's truth is all-encompassing, and a simple commandment summed up in one sentence applies to the whole gamut—those who merely insulted you, and those who abused you.

With a rapist or one-time abuser, you will never see them again and won't have to worry about this part. For me, I had to put this in practice every day because I lived with my abuser.

It may be better stated as, "Don't abuse your abuser." You are still responsible for your actions, even if they are reactions. God still expects you to be Godly, to show a Christian example, and to fight evil with good. This does NOT mean you are to be a doormat. This simply means you don't yell and scream at them, lie to them, steal from them, punch and kick them, destroy their property, blackmail them, etc. Do not try to seek revenge on them. God declares that vengeance is His alone. If you are able to live a Godly life without ever again having to interact with your abuser, choose the path that steers clear of them. If you are not, let your words and actions be governed by God. Even if your feelings are telling you to act one way, use your knowledge of the truth to overpower your feelings, and act in a way that is admirable to God.

It may come down to such simple things as saying please and thank you. Offer basic courtesy. Don't waste your energy giving them the evil eye every chance you get. Start with these small doable steps, and you will be putting action behind your decision to forgive.

The second thing is to avoid gossiping about them. The first point addressed how you talk TO them, this point addresses how you talk ABOUT them. Talking about the abuse itself is different. If you have a supportive friend, counselor, family member, or pastor who is helping you by listening to you unburden yourself, that is therapeutic, and fully allowed. What I am talking about here is verbally running them down in other areas of life. Most abuse survivors don't talk openly about their abuse, so often, people don't know that the person you're talking about hurt you so badly. But they might notice that you speak terribly about them every chance you get.

If people didn't know about the abuse, but just listened to you talk about your abuser, would they think you were the bad person, not him?

Please understand that this does not mean going to the other extreme and uttering fake compliments. You do not have to sugarcoat your abuser, or make yourself nauseous by telling false niceties about him. Simply do not insult him and degrade him in meaningless gossip to others. Don't run him down just for the sake of running him down. Trust me, it opens a door for Satan to take you further down that path of anger and bitterness, and it can override your entire decision to forgive in the first place.

If discussions about your abuser are uncomfortable, try your best to avoid them or politely get out of them. If you are forced to be there and listen, pray for strength, and just don't say anything. You don't have to be fake. But your decision to not speak ill of them will solidify your decision to forgive. You will be showing Godliness to God. Keep in mind this isn't for others. Nobody else in the conversation knows this person abused you. This is between you and God. God will be pleased and you will be strengthened when there was an opportunity for negativity to come spewing forth, and you chose not to.

I must reiterate that this does not apply to healthy counseling or unburdening yourself to a loving and compassionate listener. When talking about the abuse, speak freely. What I have been explaining here refers to innocent conversation about your abuser but not about the abuse. I am talking about gossip. That is entirely different than counseling or therapy situations.

One thing to think about is if people hear you gossiping about your abuser all the time, insulting him, or degrading him constantly, they may ask you why you hate this person so much. Are you prepared to tell them why? Gossip opens other doors. If you do want to tell people, approach them in a healthy manner and tell them in a situation that you control. Gossip is usually not such a situation. If you do not wish these people to know about the abuse, don't give them reason to wonder.

The third thing you can do to put action behind your decision to forgive is to pray for your abuser.

This is very difficult. Or at least it was for me.

I felt broken in so many areas that I wanted to spend my prayer time on me. My father certainly didn't deserve my prayer time. And he really didn't deserve anything from God. But that comes back to the whole "deserving" thing. Nothing about forgiveness is based on what someone deserves. Forgiveness is all about rising above what is deserved.

I am at the point now that I can pray, "God, please bless Dad," and mean it. I wasn't at that point for years. And God understands. You can still pray truthfully. I prayed that God would show Dad the extent of the damage he did. Only God could touch Dad's heart and reveal to him the atrocity of his sin. I prayed that Dad would learn to love me in a normal healthy way, not in a sexual way. I prayed that Dad's good traits would shine through, that I could see him being respectful and honest and hardworking and compassionate, so that I could more easily honor him the way the Bible said I must. I prayed that Dad would fall on his knees in utter revulsion of what he did, and beg the Lord for forgiveness. Just bringing your abuser to God in prayer in even the smallest way is a victory for you and a brick in your wall against Satan.

If your abuser is a stranger you'll never see again, your situation will be a little different. Praying for him will take a much different tone than if you had to maintain a relationship. One thing you can pray for is his salvation. My father was already a born-again Christian, which presented a whole different challenge. But many abusers do not know the Lord, and desperately need salvation. If your first thought is like mine, you are probably thinking that your abuser burning in hell is the only comforting thought you have. I remember thinking that I wanted to rip Dad's salvation away, so I can understand why the last thing you'd want to do is pray a horrible person INTO heaven. But think about this: Seeing their crime through God's eyes may be the only way they ever realize what they did to you.

Men who rape and beat do not think of how much they are hurting their victims. They only think about gratifying their selfish desires. If they continue along their path, they probably won't spend time grieving for what they put you through, or understanding your pain at all. But if they get saved, they will. If God enters their heart, they will be faced with the truth of what they did. They will need to seek forgiveness from God, and only then will their hearts break for the unbearable hurt they put you through. Would you rather they be callous about you forever, or come to a compassionate understanding and repentance of what they did to you?

It takes strength to forgive. It isn't easy. You may be totally convinced about the rightness of it, but daunted by how difficult it is. Give yourself realistic expectations. Know that you may not wake up tomorrow feeling totally different just because you decided today to forgive (then again you might!). Realize that it's a journey made up of many steps. Give yourself credit for every little step you take. Remember the power of your words and keep repeating out loud that you forgive your abuser. Think of it as letting him go, as if he is a boat tied to the dock that is your life, and you lift up the mooring rope and toss it into the sea, forever removing him from you. Say, "I release my abuser by forgiving him. I remove my abuser from me by forgiving him. I turn my abuser over to God by forgiving him." You do not approve of what he did, but you are casting off him and all his negativity by forgiving him.

Forgive to release.

Forgive to allow God's perfect justice to happen.

Forgive to free yourself.

Remember that forgiveness shows in how you treat people and how you talk about them, not in warm fuzzies you feel towards them. Remember that forgiveness is a decision you make, a commitment to do what God tells you, not a feeling you feel.

I will end with powerful scriptures that sum up God's message on forgiveness. They sometimes seem stark and harsh in their delivery, not softened to be palatable. That is why I wanted to thoroughly explain forgiveness first. But whether or not we understand it, whether or not we want to do it, the command to do it in God's Word supersedes everything.

He states in Matthew 5, "But I say unto you, love your enemies, bless them that curse you, do good to them that hate you, and pray for them which despitefully use you, and persecute you."

Mark 11 tells us, "And when you stand praying, if you hold anything against anyone, forgive them…"

Colossians 3 says, "Bear with each other and forgive one another…Forgive as the Lord forgave you."

In Luke, we are told, "If your brother or sister sins against you…forgive them. Even if they sin against you seven times in a day…you must forgive them."

God's Word is clear. And we know that everything He tells us to do is for our good. Open the gates of healing in your heart and watch the bitterness flow away as you are obedient to God and forgive your abuser.

Lord, help me to forgive. Thank you that you first forgave me—that you showed me how incredible a gift it is by continuing to extend it to me. Now please help me extend it to my abuser. Help me fight the battle in my mind, for that is where it will take place. I do not want to keep the negativity of my abusive experience with me, so I release it by forgiving. I release my abuser into your hands, and I leave vengeance and justice with you. I pray for your peace to flood my heart as I walk this forgiveness journey. Please let me feel the lightness and freedom that comes with forgiving. Please give me patience to keep at it, to secure my victory despite setbacks. Help me to know that my feelings do not dictate this, but rather help me strengthen my decision to forgive. I am committed to doing the right thing, and I need your help to do it. In Jesus' name, amen.

Chapter 6—Free Will

Have you ever wondered why this happened to you? Have you ever demanded a reason from God? If so, have you been given a satisfactory explanation, or any explanation at all?

I have never come across someone who got an answer on this from God. You can logistically see that you may have been victimized because you were in the wrong place at the wrong time, or you were nice to someone who took advantage of you. Or, like me, you were constantly available to someone who had vile desires and no self-control. But to answer the question of why awful abuse happens to good people—well, asking God for that answer is something I would advise not doing. He simply has a record of not answering.

It is actually comforting for me to believe that God has intelligence so far above my own that I couldn't even begin to comprehend the answers to my questions. If God said to me, "I would like to tell you the answer, but you wouldn't understand it," I'd believe Him. And I would be OK with that. What I wouldn't be OK with is deifying a God who was not smarter than I am.

If I assume that God's reasoning and logistics are something I could understand, then He is only as smart as me, and *that* doesn't deserve to be worshipped. The Bible tells us that His ways are above our ways, and further explains that no one can know the mind of the Lord. I have used this as comfort many times when things don't make sense. I tell myself, "God understands this, even if I don't." And sometimes I get even more basic than that: "God's got this" or "God is in control." If He is worth deifying, if He is worth worshipping with our entire being, if we believe He created the universe and everything in it, if we believe He is who He says He is, then obviously He is infinitely smarter than us.

But I do believe we have been given a glimpse into why bad things happen to good people. We simply don't like to apply this basic knowledge to something that is so unfair. Here it is: free will.

This is the closest I can come to giving you an explanation for why you suffered unjustly. You may think you understand free will. But bear with me—it is deeper than you may have contemplated before.

Free will is a beautiful gift from God. It is the only reason love can exist. It makes us humans, rather than robots. But like anything that has a powerful good side, it can be used powerfully for the bad too.

There are examples all around us of things that should be good, that were meant for good, now being used badly. Just look at sex. It's the greatest physical pleasure human beings can experience. But used inappropriately, it can cause immeasurable physical and mental pain, slavery, and even death. Look at something like electricity. We can't even picture our world without it. It changed a candle-dependent society into a world that can function just as well at night as during the day, and it powers a countless number of things that make our lives what they are. But if you get too close to it, it kills you instantly. It's even been used for torture.

Look at a more recent addition to our lifestyles: Facebook. How wonderful it was when it first came out. And when used properly, it's still a fun, informative way to stay connected. But used poorly, it causes scandal, depression, theft, and suicide.

I've said many times in the past few years that there isn't anything the good guys can create that the bad guys can't corrupt. Our lives are full of daily choices as to how we are going to use everything we come across. We are moral beings with constant opportunities to do the right thing or the wrong thing. That is because we have free will.

And man, are we ever attached to it.

There isn't a country on the globe that values free will like America does. We know the importance of free will more than many other people, and freedom is an inherent part of who we are. It defines us as a country, and we have died for that privilege many times.

It also defines human beings in general. Before we were divided into countries and had any constitutions to defend or wars to fight, we had free will. It was given to the very first human being, and will never be taken away.

It would be hard to even begin describing how beautiful free will is. We take it for granted. And that's not a bad thing. God understands that anything we have, constantly, every minute of every day of our lives, becomes just natural and normal. We only see the marvel of it, or glimpse the depth of its beauty, when it is taken from us.

We as Americans have freedoms granted to us by our Constitution. You can educate yourself however you want and pursue whichever career you want; you can marry whomever you choose; you can have as many children as you want; you can live anywhere you want, in whatever size and style of home you choose; you can have as many pets as you want; you can have as many bikes, cars, boats, or toys as you want; you can create your own schedule and your towns and cities don't give you curfews; you can pursue any sport, craft, hobby, or pastime you want. The list goes on and on.

But God's gift came first. God gave you the freedom inherent in being a human being. You couldn't even attempt to record the myriad of decisions you make every single day that come from free will allowing it. You chose the alarm clock that woke you up this morning. You chose the sheets on the bed you slept in. You chose to brush your teeth. You chose to wear what you wanted. And hundreds of little decisions followed those.

Just imagine if any one of those was taken from you. You experience such freedom every day. Without consciously thinking about it, you embrace your humanness by exercising your right to decide how you live—from the tiniest detail to the biggest dream. Imagine if you had to program a robot to act like a human. It could go through the physical motions of walking, getting dressed, talking, sitting and standing. You could program it to blink, swallow, laugh, and cry. But you could never program morality into it, such that it could handle the many decisions it would have to make every day.

One of the many beautiful things about free will is that love could not exist without it. Love is the greatest gift God gave us (aside from salvation), and it depends entirely on our ability to choose it. Using the robot example, we could program a robot to ACT like it was in love. It could blush, bat its eyelashes, hold hands, hug and kiss, say the right words, buy cards and flowers, and do any number of things as an outward show. But it could never FEEL love. That is part of being human.

Love has enthralled and baffled humans ever since the very beginning. Nothing else has inspired so many songs, books, or movies. Nothing else has remained, at its very core, unchanged throughout millennia of mankind's existence. Nothing has caused our hearts to soar with such pleasure, caused us to commit to a lifetime of nurturing it, caused us to bear up under arguments and emotional pain for the sake of its good parts. It never goes out of style, we never get tired of experiencing it, we never wear it out. And we still haven't figured it out, either. There is a mystery in love that only God understands, and its power to baffle us has always been part of its thrill.

And ALL that depends on free will.

Having someone love you because they want to is what love is all about. Having someone commit to you because they love you is an experience nothing else in the world can match. Without free will, love and all its beauty wouldn't even be understandable to us, let alone livable.

Let's take this beauty one step farther. I think love is the second greatest gift God gave us. The greatest is salvation. And it depends on free will too.

God chose not to create a race of beings that were forced to love Him. That's a contradiction in terms, but it's the only way to say it. God could have made creatures who fawned over Him, obeyed Him, flattered Him, and sang His praises, every day of their lives. Evidently, He knew how unfulfilling and useless that would be. Instead He created *us*. He gave us the choice to love Him back. He gave us free will, and then we get to use that free will to love Him, or deny Him. It's all up to us.

The biggest and best things in our lives depend on us having free will. God planned it that way. His Word instructs us to "choose ye this day whom you will serve." He holds out to all of us an amazing gift, in salvation, that I can't imagine why anybody wouldn't choose. But countless people don't. And God allows it. Immense numbers of souls travel the "broad path to destruction," and God honors His gift of free will by letting them. The magnitude of this gift becomes apparent when you ponder how everything we enjoy comes to us in the form of a choice. And choices are only choices because we have free will to choose.

OK, so free will is a beautiful thing. It's a gift from God. It's at the core of human existence. Now let's get a little more personal.

You have it.
Your abuser has it.

Can you understand the basic foundation of that truth?

Bad guys have free will to be bad just as much as good guys have free will to be good. The minute God reaches down and takes away that beautiful gift He gave us, that's the moment we cease to be human beings. *Would you give up your free will to make sure somebody else lost theirs?*

That is the crux of so many people's pain. Millions of people cannot wrap their minds around God "allowing" a bad person to be bad. And so their faith journey stops right there. That is a tragedy. God deserves mankind's understanding of the completeness of free will. And you certainly deserve an understanding of it, lest your faith journey grind to a halt in the presence of your perceived injustice.

Your abuser hurting you was unjust. But your abuser having free will was not unjust.

Because I want this to really sink in, I will repeat: Would you give up your free will to make sure somebody else lost theirs? Do you realize what would happen to humanity if individuals got to decide if certain other individuals kept or lost their free will? Do you think there has ever been a time in your life when someone else would have wanted you to lose your free will? Because you are human, the answer to that question is yes. There is no way you can get to human adulthood without ever having hurt someone else. So it is logical and reasonable to assert that you would be on both the taking and losing sides of free will if it were able to be individually taken away.

And therein lies God's conundrum. *Free will is all or none.* That is the only way it can be. Anything else isn't free. Anything else does not maintain God's claim that all His children are equal. As God's creation, we are all subject to the same boundaries. Free will is a gift that is given absolutely equally to every single person ever born. God cannot and will not take it back. If you have free will, you must accept that everyone else has it too.

Sin entered the world by free will. God told Adam and Eve not to eat the fruit of one tree. But He didn't physically reach down and stop them. So they exercised their "right" to do what they wanted, even when they knew it was wrong. And sin entered the world. It has been corrupting people ever since. God is not sitting up in heaven with an eraser, constantly rubbing out people's mistakes. We can all testify that we have learned from our mistakes. Nobody wants their child to touch a hot stove, and so we warn them. But just one act of experiencing the painful results of touching that stove is actually the best teacher.

Part of us still wants God to erase the really heinous things, though. Isn't there a limit? Sure, this free will sounds good, and no, we don't want to give ours up. But can't God reach down and prevent just the worst of the worst? The simple answer is no. Sex will not be taken away from us just because some people choose to use it to enslave others, torture others, or kill others. Electricity will not be banned from our lives just because misuse of it will instantly kill us. And Facebook, to revisit my three original examples, will not be shut down because some people use it irresponsibly with negative results. We put rules and regulations on things for good reason. But criminals will always exist. People will always push right past those rules to do things their way, to satisfy their own desires.

So your abuser exercised his right to free will. Plain and simple. That's the only reason we will be given on this side of heaven. It's not God's fault for not stopping him. It's God's beautiful gift that allowed him to be human.

The good news is your abuser did not turn you into a robot. He used free will wrong. But you have the same freedom and you can choose to use yours right. Would you hand over your gift of free will to your abuser? Certainly not. Well, you are doing exactly that if you let his negativity color every day for the rest of your life. If you instead choose to cut off his hold on you, redesign your future God's way, work to gain victory over your pain—you will be using free will the way God hoped His people would. Your abuser using his free will wrongly does not at all take away *your ability to use yours rightly.*

Lord, thank you for the gift of free will. Thank you that you gave that gift to everyone, and will never take it away. Thank you that it allows us to love each other, to love you, and to choose salvation. Help me to remember that free will makes me human. Help me to understand that your plan for humanity cannot work if you take back free will. Please help me to use my free will to do the right thing. Thank you that I am as free to do right as my abuser was free to do wrong. Help me to constantly choose to do right. Help me to understand the magnitude of my freedom, to embrace it fully, to be thankful for it, and to use it to overcome the negativity in my life. Using my free will, I choose victory! In Jesus' name, amen.

TAKE BACK YOUR PEARLS

Chapter 7—Pity, Power, Parking, and Pain

Here, I want to examine some principles that will help you on your journey. Your abuser dumped a lot of negativity into your life. And now it's up to you to get it out. Sometimes I picture myself with a shovel, digging out the bad stuff and throwing it away, one shovelful at a time. The principles in this chapter will help you do just that.

Because I got hit with this realization and then later wondered why I didn't automatically know it, I will assume some of you don't automatically know it either. Walking the Christian path takes work. It's such a life changing experience to give your heart to God, to become saved. It may be easy to believe that now that you've arrived, the hard part is over. You just secured your salvation, you are going to heaven, you found the truth, your heart is soaring, life will be better now.

But that's just the beginning. That's just entrance. Life will be better, but you'll have to work at it. God gives you the tools—He doesn't do it for you.

Simply getting saved is like getting a gym membership. You have entrance ability. But you will not be one iota more fit if you never go to that gym and work out. How many of you have membership with God, but haven't used it? Your victory, your peace, your happiness is in *living* for God, not just making that one-time decision. You can't then sit back and do nothing. You could still get to heaven. But you will live a miserable life before you do.

Salvation is not a promise of a victorious life. The Bible would be one chapter if that's all there was. The reality is that there's our salvation way over on one side, and our arrival in heaven way over on the other side. That big chunk in the middle is called LIFE, and it's only as good as we let it be. We must grow in the Lord, we must progress, or we will not be happy. There is no comfortable neutrality; we will stagnate without purposeful growth. I know because I did. Your entrance into heaven and a happy life are two different things. *One does not come with the other.*

Be sure you have a grasp of this fundamental principle. Your salvation alone will save you from hell, but not from life. Be prepared to put in effort. By now you're probably realizing that overcoming something as big as sexual abuse is a hard journey. It requires effort every day. It requires effort into your thoughts, beliefs, and actions. It's hard. But it's so worth it. Your salvation is a beautiful foundation. Build a beautiful life on top of that. It won't build itself.

I just want to stress that truth because the principles I'm going to discuss here are hard. They require undoing defaults. They require putting daily effort into thinking differently, so that you can behave differently. It's hard to shovel a giant pile of manure out of your life. And again, I realize it's unfair. But if you do nothing, the pile of manure stays in your life. Fair or not, you're the one holding the shovel.

One of the things that hit me really hard in my own journey was pity versus power. You can have pity, or you can have power. *But you cannot have both.*

It hit me hard because I realized I had been living on the pity side. I felt sorry for myself. I knew the world would feel sorry for me too, if it knew. And I realized there was power in that. Or so I thought. It was like I was owed a debt, and I could bring up my story at any time to try to collect that debt. How this played out, and what it eventually taught me, was that the power I thought I had was just negative influence. Power, true power, lies in letting go of the pity.

Once I began to grasp this, I saw it so strongly in my sister. She thrived on the pity. Her self-pity opened doors for her in her mind. Poor her, she had been so mistreated, surely she should be allowed to ... fill in the blank here, that's what she did. She used pity to cover other sins. Pity was an excuse. Pity was a crutch. She couldn't see that leaning on that crutch and limping through life was keeping her from overcoming. It was keeping her UNDER. But it felt good.

One thing that makes it really hard to let go of pity is that the world will feed it. The world will gladly give you that crutch. You will have a constant excuse at your disposal to throw out any time you want. You will get "understanding" from the world if you use your bad experiences to justify bad behavior. How many times have you heard a news story about a criminal, where investigation into his background showed trouble, instability, or abuse in his past? "He did this bad thing because bad things were done to him." Do you ever find yourself thinking, *Well it's no wonder, then, it makes sense*? Do you ever go so far as to think, *Well, it's OK, then*? What kind of a horrible vicious cycle would life be if badness perpetuated badness and we allowed it? Well, in a kind of mental tolerance, the world does allow it.

But you won't get that from God. God wants to take away that crutch, and teach you to walk on your own again. And fair warning—you won't get understanding from the world when you do this. You will have to mentally tell yourself that God's support is more important than the world's support. They don't naturally go hand in hand, and this will be a choice for you. Do you want to walk in victory or limp in pity?

What I am talking about here is a mindset. It's not an action. But know that overcoming abuse is a battle that is fought in your mind. Enjoyment of life comes from having peace and joy on the inside. Those are hard to have with that giant pile of manure hanging around. Once your peace and joy are firmly in place on the inside, manifestations of them will show on the outside. The battle is not won by trying really hard to change your behavior. The battle is won by changing how you think. Then the behavior follows naturally.

So let go of your pity. Stop feeling sorry for yourself. Yes, what happened to you is bad. Know that sympathy would be there, in a healthy sense, from anyone who knew and understood your pain. Know that God's heart breaks for you in that way. But decide that you don't want to stay in that place of tears. That title is called "Victim." Throw off that title and aim for the new title of Overcomer.

You'll have to give up your "get out of jail free" card. You'll have to decide that your power to choose is more important than your ability to have a world-accepted excuse for wrong actions. I'm sure you have tasted, even a little, the freedom the world gives by readily blaming your sins on somebody else. It's intoxicating. You don't have to bear responsibility.

Poor abused you, your sins are somebody else's fault. Satan would love you to get hooked on this false power, to keep you chained down to pity. I want you to see the power you have in CHOICE. I want you to see what you're giving up if you deny your choice. And blaming your current actions on your past abuse, like my sister did, says that you are giving up your power to choose. The minute you say you are free from blame because you didn't have a choice, *you give up any power you have to choose to change your course in life*. If you are just waiting for the world to line up right and start treating you well, the same way it lined up wrong and treated you badly, you will be waiting forever and you will have a miserable life. You must choose to heal, to overcome, to have your victory.

Hanging onto pity also keeps you hanging onto your past. No matter what good things God tries to introduce into your life, pity keeps that overriding dark cloud coloring everything. It seeps into every facet of your existence, without your actually applying it. If it's living permanently in your heart, it will touch everything else.

Tell pity it has to leave. You had a pitiful past. But draw the line now. The future can be as bright and victorious as you let it. Pity will only constantly tell you to look back, to remember the bad, to wallow in the painful things. Cutting off pity is like cutting off the ankle chain that ties you to a prison wall.

Declare out loud that you do not feel sorry for yourself anymore. Pray that God helps you banish your feelings of self-pity. As you do that, as you close that door, you will be opening another. You will be allowing power to take its place.

There is so much power in God's ways! God is living in you, and you have access to all that He is. There is power in stomping on negativity. Remember that only positive can beat negative, we fight evil with good. That's because the good has the power. There is no power in pity. Look in your life at anyone who constantly wallows in pity. There is no power in that life. There is only negative feelings. Don't be that person. When you let go of pity, God doesn't just leave you standing there with nothing. He is waiting to pour power into your life. Remember that power and pity cannot exist together. So the more you give up pity, the more power you invite in.

All the things we've been talking about—knowing who you are in Christ, letting go of guilt and condemnation, forgiving, understanding free will—they all stomp out pity. The more you do all these things, the more of yourself you are giving over to God's power, and the less of yourself you are giving over to pity. Pity will not thrive when you chase after God's truth. Pity is starved when you declare the Word of the Lord, when you pray asking for the Godly tools He has promised you, when you state to yourself and God that you want to do the right thing, even though it's hard. Identifying pity, and deliberately casting it down, is another step in that victorious direction.

I had to decide that I did not want those mushy-gushy self-gratifying feelings that the world would give me when I told my sorrowful story. I felt like God was asking me, "What if nobody ever felt sorry for you again?" So I will ask it to you.

Would you be OK with that? What if nobody knew about your abuse, and you were expected by the world to live your life like anybody else? What if all your words and actions were judged by the same standards and expectations as a normal person with a healthy past? Do you really want that? Or do you want the lesser standards, more lenient expectations, and soothing platitudes that the world would give you if you let pity stay rooted?

Aim high! Reach for power. Let go of pity.

Don't park at the point of your pain. Hanging onto pity puts our lives in park. We stop moving forward. We can't take in new truths because everything goes through the filter of pity and pity keeps us down, wallowing and bogging. We stagnate. Then we start going backwards. No parking!

Remember I said there is no such thing as neutrality with God? If you are not moving forward, you will not stay at a healthy, neutral place. The world (and Satan) will chip away at you and fill in those voids that are created as you progress through life without taking God with you. You must meaningfully put and keep God at the helm of your life. No parking. Staying where your pain put you is exactly where Satan wants you. No progress, no growth, no victory. All pain, all despair, all hopelessness. How long have you been parked at the point of your pain?

I fell into despair because I parked. God steers a moving ship. God is your rudder, but if the ship is not moving, the rudder is useless. Don't let your abuser put a brick wall across the road of your life and say, "Here you will stay." All those miles of future road—gone. You would never deliberately do this. Your abuser doesn't deserve that power and influence. Yet that's exactly what you are doing if you stay parked where he put you. If you refuse to take the hard journey of healing, then your abuser wins. He got your past, he's getting your present, and you're giving him your future. Take it back!

The world cannot give you what you are owed from your abuse. The world cannot pay that debt. You could spend your whole life fighting to satisfy the sense of justice that burns inside you. And you won't be able to do it. *Only God can*. I'm not saying you should give up on justice. Just the opposite in fact: leave justice to God. Put it where it belongs. We have seen the mess the world can make of it anyway. Our justice system is sorely lacking in justice. Why should McDonald's be sued because their coffee is hot? Why should O.J. Simpson get away with murder? Why should a robber be able to sue the owners of the house he was robbing because he slipped on the ice? Only God gives pure justice. And He says in His Word that He will. Trust Him to do it.

I realized that I was expecting something of my father. If I had thought deeply about it, I would have understood that he could not give me back the childhood he stole from me. He couldn't change my negative feelings and defaults into positive ones. He couldn't fix me. But my emotions screamed loudly inside me—he owes me something.

If nothing else, I wanted him to face some of the knowledge of what he did. I was glad to leave home and not be living under his roof anymore. But there he was, continuing in a successful life with no consequences or repercussions for his sin. Surely, he could at least acknowledge that he hurt me. And then I wanted an apology.

I prayed about it, and then I wrote him a letter. I explained in it how what he did to me left me scarred and scared. I told him that because of him, I hated the male anatomy. I pictured chopping up penises with chainsaws. How was I ever going to be a good wife someday? Did he realize the damage he had done to me?

I went home and personally delivered the letter. He read it, but stayed silent. He hung his head and wouldn't look me in the eye. Finally, he said he was sorry. Then he walked out of the room.

That was it.

I had given justice my best shot. I was brutally honest with him about what he had done. I had forced him to say he was sorry. He didn't sound like he meant it. And I didn't feel healed.

God was patient and gentle with me as I mourned this. He brought me to the realization that only He can heal me. I had to completely let go of any assumption I had that Dad would do it. I will admit that it felt good to tell some of those things to Dad. And that can definitely be part of your healing. I later encouraged my sister to do it and it helped her. It's one of the things we can do to address the human part of us and what our humanness needs. But it's not the biggest step, and it won't bring about your victory on its own.

You are in control of what you say and do to someone else. I was in control of writing that letter to Dad. But you are not in control of what that other person does after that. Be sure you see the therapeutic value in just doing your part. Be sure you don't base the therapeutic value of the situation on what your abuser says or does in response. By the time I explained this to my sister, years after I had written my own letter, I was able to see it in a far better light. She was able to let go of certain things just by writing them down and giving them to Dad. End of story. It was in *not expecting anything from Dad after* that allowed it to be a good thing.

Your abuser will not heal you because he simply can't.

Dad had no desire to revisit his sin. I can't imagine anyone in those shoes wanting to sit down and hash out the negative affect his actions have done to someone else over the years. Even if your abuser was willing to hear you out, talk freely about it, say all the right words, and give you a heartfelt apology, that wouldn't heal you. It might help you, and I would rejoice with anyone who got that result. But you are still left with the injustice of a stolen childhood, defaults you have to change, repulsive thoughts you have to beat down. Some of you are left with infections, diseases, malfunctioning bodies, pregnancies—even sincere remorse from the perpetrator cannot erase these things.

You must fully understand that your abuser, and the world around you, will not repay the debt you are owed. There is no cosmic balance scale that will even out the wrongs done to you, no matter how much you have heard about karma. I'm sure when you read this, you are telling yourself that you get it, you aren't expecting the world to fix you. But are you? If you don't fully acknowledge your own power to bring about your healing with God's help, then you could be falling into the trap of believing, on some level, that the world will eventually fix you. Or time will. Or distance from your abuser. Or mind over matter. Or submissive acceptance. None of these things can match the complete incredible life-changing victory God has in store for you.

I say all of this to encourage you not to stay parked at the point of your pain. I want to light a fire under you, get you energized about your journey. I want to abolish all the false reasoning you may have for staying in your comfort zone, and doing nothing. I want you to chase your victory.

You must be holding God's hand throughout this whole journey. You don't have to feel strong enough to do it on your own. You're not. Remember that as you are doing your part, God is doing His. This brings me to another big choice you have to make.

God can either be your comfort or your blame, but not both.

Many people are not running to God because they are too busy blaming Him. Please, *please* don't do that. It is not God's fault that bad things happened to you. He is right there waiting, with open arms, to give you supernatural comfort and help. What an amazing gift to give up, just so you can heap blame on Him.

When the three Hebrew children were thrown into the fiery furnace for refusing to bow down to a false god, their statement declared that "our God is able to save us." There is the crux of it—God is *able*. I found that knowing God is able and seeing that He didn't is sometimes worse than thinking He isn't able. We must not get stuck on that. Yes, God is able. God can do anything. But He doesn't bow to our whims. Why did the Holocaust happen? Why are children murdered? Why does human trafficking still exist? As I said before, God's gift of free will is the closest I've come to explaining these difficult questions. God is not going to reach down and erase any potential negative or damaging thing in your life. He never promised to. Don't let that be the reason you don't go to Him for comfort.

Nobody and nothing in this world can help you like God can. There is incredible power in God working through you that you simply cannot find anywhere else. You can't change yourself on a foundational level just by trying hard. But God can. Nothing in this world will give you supernatural tools. But God has!

At any point in your journey, you may find yourself blaming God. You may question faith, or prayer, or other spiritual things, because they didn't work like you thought they would. Let God continue to teach you. Don't let Satan harden your heart at any step so that you park. Remember, no parking. Decide that you will move forward, no matter how much things don't make sense. Always remember that somebody so much wiser than you is offering you help. The person who takes the clumsiest stumbling step is better than the person who stands still and refuses to move.

I want to stress again that giving up pity to get God's power is an exchange. And it is the most crucial exchange in the whole idea of taking back your pearls. The whole journey is important, but from my experience, this one aspect is crucial, crucial, crucial. Think of it as exchanging pity for power, or exchanging dime-store pearls for real ones, or exchanging ashes for beauty—whatever makes you see the truth of it in your mind. You MUST make this exchange.

Oh, the power waiting for you! I have a hard time putting into words how amazing is the power you will receive! This is NOT an even exchange. God is waiting to give you something so life-changing! God's power allows you to feel joy, untainted by the constant spears of pain that attack you now. God's power allows you to have great relationships, have peace in your heart, sleep better at night, get rid of stomach cramps, say goodbye to anxiety, truly enjoy sex, countless real-life things that will make your journey incredible. It all comes with God's power.

The Bible talks about power to trample snakes and scorpions. I believe that is figurative, so I would never encourage you to literally do that. But if we of soft human flesh can trample something with sharp fangs and stingers and poison, then we must be using power beyond our human capabilities. This is the power God is waiting to give you, power to trample out the evil of your abuse, power to cut its ties to you, stop it affecting you, stomp it out forever. It's not that your memory will be erased and you won't even know it happened; rather it will be like it's a limp lifeless thing, there but utterly powerless.

That's how I see my abuse. It happened to me. It was really bad. But I can now talk about it, freely, without bursting into tears. I can converse to the deepest depths of it without being overtaken by feelings of anger and injustice. I can talk about it like I talk about what I'm having for dinner—it is just a subject now, removed of its power to hurt me.

I will leave you with one final analogy on this subject. Satan's power to keep you hooked on pity, constantly despairing and stagnating, and God's power to heal you, bringing peace and joy—are both power. They are drastically different, but because they're both power, their similarities can be confusing. Think of them both as pills. Little white round pills. We take pills trusting that they will heal us. We don't see the healing in them; we simply believe they are medicine, and so we swallow them. Satan's pill is just flour and water. God's pill is penicillin. Satan's pill will do nothing, and your human nature will keep indulging itself as human natures do. God's pill will eradicate your infection and save your life. What a difference!

Lord, thank you that you are helping me every little step of the way. Thank you that you don't expect me to do this on my own, and that when my strength and resources run out, you are right there filling in the gaps. Help me to break the pattern of pity in my life. I declare that I don't want self-pity. I willingly lay it down. I know what happened to me was bad, but I don't want pity to rob me of my future. Help me to control my thoughts every time I feel sorry for myself. Help me to let go of the crutch of lesser standards that the world gives me because of my abuse. I choose your power over pity! Flood my heart and mind and life with your power. I know you are able to do anything, but I do not blame you for what happened to me. Help me to leave justice to you. Thank you that you are in control and you still mete out perfect justice, even if our own legal system does not. I declare to you that I don't expect healing from my abuser or from the world. But I do expect it from you. I put my hand in yours, every day, and I ask you to help me. Empower me to take each step on my healing journey. Strengthen me if I ever park, and keep me constantly moving towards complete victory. In Jesus' name, amen.

Chapter 8 — Tools In Our Toolbox

God's Word is full of advice. It's our instruction book on life. He is the creator, we are the creation. He is the only one who can tell us how we truly function, and therefore how best to live our lives. And, thankfully, He does.

Sometimes, all that advice can sound like a bunch of rules. I found it easier to think of those nuggets as tools. God did not intend that we be overwhelmed by a flood of do's and don'ts hanging over us at all times. Rather, he gave us tools, unique help for different situations. And they are at our disposal to pick up and use as needed.

We need to be prepared to use the tools in our Spiritual Tool Box. They are instruments that help us accomplish tasks. Picture a hammer or a wrench. They aren't much good if they just sit there. But if we pick them up and use them for the purpose they were intended, they accomplish big things. The same truth holds for our spiritual tools. We have steadfastness, tenacity, perseverance, self-control, obedience, work ethic, patience, and countless others.

We need God's help for this entire journey. He will provide it in any number of ways. It's already a huge help just knowing that if we are born again, we possess this tool box. Even if I don't know how to use them all, if I'm sent to a job knowing I'm fully equipped, I already have more confidence.

I spent years not knowing what I possessed. This caused me to miss out, to pray wrong, and to feel weaker. This is where

God's Word is so important. I said at the beginning of this book that we had to believe God's Word. Well, one step before that is we have to read God's Word. It has to be part of us, because that is how He delivers so much of His help. To continue with my analogy, I spent years asking God for a hammer He had already given me. Had I known, I would have stopped asking for it and instead asked for help using it, and I would have at least tried to pick it up and give it a swing.

To illustrate what I mean, one way this showed in my life was to pray constantly that God would be with me. It was almost a generic way to include God in all my requests. "Lord, be with me as I go to this interview …" "Lord, please be with me during Dad's visit …" When there was nothing specific, my morning prayers would be filled with "God, be with me as I go about my day …"

God understood, and wasn't offended. But those were ineffective prayers. As we mature spiritually, we need to be as effective as we can in our Christian walk. We move from babies to adults, from the milk of the Word to the meat of the Word, from salvation truths to kingdom truths. It's just like going from kindergarten to twelfth grade. We learn more knowledge and skills, and we become better at being productive human beings.

God already says in His Word that he is constantly with us. That is one of His promises that brings great comfort. "I will never leave you nor forsake you." He is "an ever present help in trouble." We don't need to spend years asking God for something he gave us already. God never goes back on His Word, and so His presence with us is something we can absolutely count on. Our prayer time is better used asking for other things. He does tell us to be thankful and always have grateful hearts. I changed my prayer to, "Thank you for always being with me." It's a small thing, but because it's repeated so often, it creates pathways in our hearts and minds, and those lead to bigger things.

Speaking of gratitude, that is one of our tools. I'm sure you are already aware of it, and what Scripture says about it. But thinking of it as a tool gives it power. We can use these instructions of God to accomplish things, to help us fight battles, to change us and empower us. They're not just things we should do. They are powerful tools!

When we are first given a big gift, or receive a favor, we are naturally thankful. It is normal that we would express thanks to the giver. But God wants us to be thankful in all situations, and that includes those that don't feel good. The way we use gratitude as a tool is to wield it when we don't feel like it. When you are feeling down, find something to be thankful for. And speak it out loud to God. Even if it doesn't instantly make you feel better, it makes God feel better. It pleases Him when we do what He asks. And our love for Him should make us want to please Him.

Even worldly people acknowledge that counting your blessings is a positive exercise. And it's helpful when you're feeling down. Do it when you're sad, angry, jealous, frustrated. It flows naturally when you're happy, so by all means, let it flow then. But its therapeutic value happens when you need it to pull you up. It honestly doesn't always make me *feel* better, but it makes me *know* better. Feelings are not facts, and they are very fickle. So don't worry if you can't get your feelings where you'd like them. State the facts anyway: thank the Lord for everything good that is in your life. And especially if you've been praying about something specific, thank the Lord that He is working on it. Know that no prayer is ignored by God, and He does so much on our behalf behind the scenes. Acknowledge that.

As you read the Bible, be on the lookout for tools. There are many of them, and I won't go over all of them. I just want to center on a few to explain my point. But remember to think of God's instructions as help for us, not burdensome rules or restrictions.

Self-control is one of the tools God has already given us if we're born again. If you think you can't control your thoughts and actions, think again. Having an abusive past does not mean you get to be abusive, or be sexually immoral, or treat others badly. And again, the world says it does. The world will give you a break on this whole self-control thing because of your past. God won't. This tool may be lying dormant in your life, but it's there. Recognizing that is equivalent to picking it up. Ask God for help to use it. Thank Him that He gave you a valuable and relevant help in life. And never give up trying to apply it.

If self-control isn't part of your natural personality, don't expect a miracle change overnight. Any craft that requires tools also requires a learning curve to use them. Speak out loud, "I do have self-control. I can decide to do or not do something. I am not at the whim of my desires, or anyone else's opinions." Seeing negative defaults in ourselves can be discouraging. But God is a pattern-breaker! Don't let a habit derail you just because it's entrenched. Use the tool of self-control to start taking back leadership of all your faculties.

The armor that God speaks of in His Word is a tool for us as well. Ephesians tells us to "put on the full armor of God," and just like tools, armor is useless if we do nothing with it. Know that you possess it and start learning to use it. Take, for example, the breastplate of righteousness. A breastplate protects you, so when arrows and swords are being thrown at you, they bounce off and you don't get hurt. Knowing who you are in Christ, that you have righteousness through Him, will deflect anything Satan throws at you. "You're a slut," "You're like this because of him," "You'll never change," "You are tainted forever." Those accusations from the enemy can pierce your heart, get right into your soul, and dictate who you think you are and, therefore, how you act. Or they can bounce off. It all depends on if you put on your breastplate. And putting on your breastplate means acknowledging and accepting the gift of righteousness God gave you.

I recommend reading this entire chapter in Ephesians and learning about the whole suit of armor God has gifted us. He has definitely prepared us for battle!

One thing I've decided is a tool is choice. It may not sound like it, but I've come to that conclusion because it's there for us, just like all our other tools, but we have to pick it up and use it properly. We talked about free will in a previous chapter, and this may be another way to say the same thing. But I want you to visualize these nuggets as tools, so you can see yourself picking one up anytime, and deliberately deciding to use it to improve your life.

If you are like me, you feel like choice was ripped away from you. You had no choice in your abuse, and you learned to silently accept and tolerate. And then you probably subconsciously learned that your choices aren't really yours. You were powerless, your abuser got to make the decisions, your will and your desires were trampled and didn't matter. That's the bad news.

The good news is—you are in control now. You get to decide! Take back every speck of choice that was stolen from you. Determine that you refuse any longer to give your choices to anyone else. And I think the first thing you should choose is happiness. That's right, you get to CHOOSE happiness. You don't have to wait for it to happen to you. It truly is your decision. This gives you power. Psalms tell us "happy is the man whose God is the Lord." It doesn't say you're happy if you have no pain, or if you're rich, or if you are married, or have children. You can choose happiness just because God offers it. Period. You can choose happiness just because you're a child of God. Joy and contentment are His gifts. *The amount of negativity in your past does not at all control the amount of happiness in your future.*

Of course, our circumstances dictate some happiness. God understands that happiness wanes when sickness appears, or we lose a job, or a friend hurts us. Countless things can affect our happiness. But isn't it wonderful that our free will can affect it too? Choosing it is something we can do to combat and eventually overcome all the circumstances that the world thinks are the only determining factors.

An interesting study of lottery winners showed that extreme happiness doesn't last past six months. We "level out." We get used to whatever is normal and regular, and it ceases to bring us extreme happiness anymore. If you know the wisdom of not saying, "I'll be happy when I win the lottery," then apply the same wisdom to not saying, "I'll be happy when my pain is gone." Decide to be happy during the process—it's yours for the taking.

Apply the same technique to this that you've applied elsewhere. Speak it out loud. You don't have to wait to feel it. In God's economy, stating the fact comes first and the feeling comes later. Say out loud, "I choose happiness today. Thank you Lord that you are my God, and you have given me the freedom to choose. I choose to be happy."

Once you grasp the power of choice, you can use it for other things that are life-changing. We have already talked about forgiveness. Here, I will just state that forgiveness is a choice. We don't wait until we feel like it, or our abuser has asked for it, or the effects of the abuse seem to be wearing off. We choose to do it because God wants us to, and because He gave us the power to choose it. If forgiveness itself feels too daunting to tackle, think of choice as the tool—pick it up and start chipping away at forgiveness.

Love can also be a choice. Anybody who has been married a while can attest to that. The wonderful fluttery feelings that accompany it are part of it. Indeed they are a gift from God, and some of the most enjoyable moments life will ever give you. But the people we love the most are the ones who have the most power to hurt us. After all, they have our hearts.

Using our tool of choice means love can be sustained, even when the fluttery feelings have taken a sabbatical.

Dear God, thank you that you have equipped me with spiritual tools to help me in life. Thank you that they are mine, just for believing in you. Help me to be diligent in reading your Word and learning what my tools are. And then help me to use them. Even if I don't feel it, thank you that you have already given me self-control, perseverance, steadfastness, choice, and many others. Help me to apply these tools to my journey of healing over my abuse. I have so much to be thankful for, and I give you gratitude, even in the midst of my pain. In Jesus' name, amen.

Chapter 9 — I've Done It: Now What?

My hope is that you will read this book many times. And not necessarily in order. Read the chapters over again that you are struggling with. This whole book can be read in a matter of hours, but it will take a lot longer than that to consistently apply everything in a life-changing way. It took me years just to see myself the way God does—a beautiful child of Him, a unique creation, fearfully and wonderfully made. And then even longer to believe that my righteousness in Him was a steadfast unchanging forever promise, one that I could count on to be stronger than any darts Satan threw at me.

Take as much time as you need to fully grasp each truth. Let it go from head knowledge to heart knowledge. Let it go from words to actions. Whether it is knowing who you are in Christ, letting go of guilt, forgiving, letting go of pity, understanding free will—let God help you build these truths into impenetrable fortresses in your soul. Feel free to stay on one "project" until you have gained victory. It will become a building block, upon which other victories will be placed.

What I am going to talk about in this chapter is best tackled when you feel you have achieved a firm grasp of the previous chapters. This material covers an "onward and upward" mentality that seeks an even higher victory, and will bring you to true overcomer status. However, it can seem quite unpalatable if you have not fully embraced the steps preceding it.

I remember first wanting that "something more," and it felt wonderful. It signified healing. I was no longer bogged in the process of just getting over the pain. I felt like I had fought my way back to the "normal" life I assumed everybody else was living. And I wanted to build on that. I was not content with just normal or ordinary. I did not want to merely survive. I wanted to thrive.

If we keep our hand firmly placed in God's, and strive for spiritual maturity our whole lives, we will constantly be on that onward and upward journey. There is no point in human life when we can stop and look around and declare that we have arrived. There will always be more steps to take. And so I will continue leading you towards peace in your heart and joy in your life. We have removed a lot of negative. Now let's start adding some positive. Let's not stay at neutral—let's move on to fantastic.

The first nugget I want to advise you to do is understand feelings, and put them in their proper place. I've already mentioned this in past chapters, but I want to dig a little deeper here, and take it to a more victorious level. Feelings are not facts. *You must not make the mistake of believing your feelings.* I know that sounds crazy or backwards, but the truth of it is undeniable.

I have come to think feelings are icing on the cake of life. They make us human, not robots. They can be wonderful. They can change whatever actions we are doing, whatever we are seeing or hearing or experiencing, whatever our surroundings are—everything can be colored over with feelings. And God does mean for us to enjoy them. He never intended us to be sterile emotionless beings. But we have all seen cases of temper tantrums, or drama gone wild. Terrible things have been done from the impulsivity of intense feelings. Like everything in life, God wants us to achieve a balance with our feelings.

They cannot control us. They are not the masterminds. They are not the intelligent part. They must bow to our will, our wisdom, our spirituality. Feelings can appear much bigger than anything else, because they inherently loom large. However, we need to declare the truth. And we need to acknowledge that power and health lie in the facts of the truth, not in what we happen to be feeling. The beauty of God's system is that the right feelings do come. Proper balanced feelings that allow us to enjoy life to the fullest do come when we have laid the foundation of truth first.

We have already talked about guilt, but it's a good example to illustrate this point too. Just because you *feel* guilt doesn't mean you *are* guilty. Knowing the truth of God's Word allows you to banish that feeling. Declare that you are not guilty, and refuse to accept the condemnation that feeling brings. Do the same with ugliness, insufficiency, inadequacy, and other negative feelings. They are not facts. They do not get to define you. Recognize them immediately, speak against them, and refuse to indulge them in your mind.

You may also feel positive feelings, that need equally to be understood and put in their place. Self-justification tells you you deserve things because you've been hurt, and allows you to behave poorly but be justified in your mind. Recognize this as a feeling, not a fact. God holds a higher standard outlined in His word—reach for that, knowing that it applies to everyone regardless of past abuse.

Feeling sexy and wanting to express it can bring temporary pleasure. Abuse survivors often use sexuality inappropriately because they have been taught and wired to do so. Sexuality can be a currency that you've learned to use in exchange for favors, acceptance, or praise. Recognize this as a feeling, not a fact. That kind of sexual gratification is not permanent, not meaningful, and not from God. Use the truth that sex was created to be a beautiful thing in its proper context, and refuse to participate in it in any lesser tainted way.

Think about what your feelings are leading you to. If they lead only to despair and to self-hate, or temporary pleasure that comes with conviction, they are destructive and not of God. If they lovingly lead you to change your course in a better direction, fix something that is wrong, understand something in a new light, etc., then they are productive. Satan uses feelings as weapons against you to keep you down, bogged and floundering in negativity. Constantly use God's truth as a weapon in return, to control feelings and allow them to be the wonderful icing on life's cake that God intended.

A second nugget that is a positive life changer is basically to just believe what God says in Romans. But pay close attention to the wording. Romans 8:28, a very comforting verse and a foundation of our faith, says God will work everything together for good. It doesn't say that things will always automatically BE good. It means all the pieces of your life, good and bad, work TOGETHER to make something amazing. Flour on its own is disgusting to eat, and so is baking soda, sugar, raw eggs, corn oil, and salt. But if you put it all together, it makes a cake. And that is delicious. The end result is so much more than the sum of its parts. That's how God works with our lives. He takes everything and mixes it TOGETHER to make something good.

The world could never do that. The world has no master engineer like God. What a beautiful promise God gives us! Just like everything else, it depends on a healthy balance and a reverence for who God is. We cannot just do anything we want, and then count on God to wave a magic wand over it and make it good. But when we are trying our best, and planting and sowing seeds of positivity in our lives, we open the door for God's work to manifest powerfully.

Note the condition—you must love the Lord. The actual verse says, "And we know that all things work together for good to them that love God, to them who are called according to His purpose." God always does His part, and He expects us to do ours. Sometimes our part is as simple as just believing. What a generous exchange! Don't underestimate the importance of doing your part though. Don't let any setbacks take you away from your goal of loving and believing God with all your heart. Remember, these promises in His Word are for YOU. Not somebody better or luckier. You.

I have mentioned this before, but it bears repeating here. Do not ask God why. Don't let the quest of seeking reasons that make sense to you be the stumbling block that keeps you from moving on. God does not want your trust in Him to depend on your understanding of Him. People who get tripped up on asking why usually feel like they are banging their heads against a brick wall. God rarely answers that question; He simply waits patiently for us to give up our selfish desire to have life make sense, and pick up our cross and resume our journey.

People who get tripped up on asking why are usually standing still on their spiritual journey. They are not taking steps to progress. They are stuck. They are mired in one place, and have decided that they cannot move on until a reason releases them to journey again. Beware the risk of that. Realize you may be sacrificing your entire future to stand in that one place, banging down heaven's doors for an answer God does not intend to give. Only God knows why I had to suffer my entire childhood. But I trust God. He knows all the details, and I do not. He will make something good come of it. And my inner strength now, the mightier person I have become, is part of that good.

A third nugget to present to you is indeed a difficult one: Try to see the other person's point of view. This pertains to any situation in life that could be troubling, and is a key to happiness in general if you can master it. It's so applicable because life absolutely will present you with people who irritate you. If you get cut off in traffic, imagine that person is on their way to the hospital, or is crying so hard they can't see the road. Has that ever been you? Take the time to be happy that you're not in that same rush. We're in a politically rife time right now and people will vehemently disagree with you on foundational concepts. Try to accept that they honestly love the country too, and in their own very different way, want what's best. Ladies, give your husband the benefit of the doubt—is he really trying to ruin your day, or is he just from Mars?

Now, here's the tough one: Can you see anything at all from your abuser's perspective? Your abuser is not a happy, healthy person. That may not matter to you, but just think—you can be. You can live a life that is so much better than theirs it will put them to shame. This doesn't mean you understand why they abused you, or you see its entirety from their point of view. Truthfully, all it did for me was reveal that my abuser was in the grip of something so negative and evil he couldn't possibly be happy.

Remember, God is the master architect. God made humans, and he gets to make the rules on how they function. Evil cannot produce real happiness. Your abuser cruelly taking what he wants against another's will absolutely cannot produce the good fruit of happiness or peace or joy. It is impossible. Remember, God wrote the software. Satan does not get to rewrite it. He can only fool selfish and gullible people into buying his lies.

Personally, a little bit of competitiveness did me good in this area. I felt like I could rise higher than my abuser, I could have something he could never have: foundational happiness. In other words, I could be better than him. Some may argue that is not a good motivational tactic. I say you are absolutely allowed to trample evil by declaring you will be better. Staying upset at your abuser, withholding forgiveness, letting the flame of rage burn against him forever—this all just keeps you down at his level. Remember that only good can overcome evil. So pursuing your own happiness the way God outlines will leave your abuser in the dust. No matter how successful his life appears, if he has not repented, he is not happy. But you can be.

Romans 15:13 says, "May the God of hope fill you with all joy and peace in believing, so that you may overflow with hope by the power of the Holy Spirit." Note how we are told that peace and joy come from believing. It's almost too easy to be true. But again, what a generous exchange! Don't miss out on it. Your abuser committed heinous actions to try to satisfy something in himself, to bring happiness. I guarantee it didn't work. But all you have to do is believe. You can do it anywhere, anytime, just between you and God. You can ignore whatever negative feelings might be getting in the way, and use your free will to choose to believe. And what do you get in return? Happiness!

The fourth nugget requires even more deep digging into yourself. Yes, these are getting harder! But the rewards are also getting bigger. I challenge you to ask yourself: What is YOUR part in your situation? That may seem cruel, because you were victimized, and believe me I know that. So does God. You are not to blame for what happened to you. But what are you doing now to perpetuate a lifestyle that your abuse started?

For example, I became a huge flirt. I realized, much later in life when I was seeking spiritual maturity, that I had dealt with unwanted male attention my entire life. I think at the beginning I liked it. I honestly can't remember my exact mindset except to say that I was messed up. But I had no tools to differentiate good from bad male attention. My father had ruined that. I had to reconcile a loving, Christian father with horrid physical treatment, and that ruined my ability to disconnect those two in the future. So I let men take advantage of me.

I didn't get raped or anything like that, but they did go too far, and I let them. When I finally wondered why I attracted guys who put me in the situation of having to kick them out of my life because of their inappropriate behavior, God gently showed me that I had a part in it. I had to consciously work at changing the way I sexually behaved with men. And the thing was, I didn't even know I was doing it. I needed God to SHOW me, then HELP me. And He did. I learned to nip it in the bud.

But if you stay stuck at the point where you are blaming your abuser, feeling sorry for yourself, harboring anger, and railing against injustice, you will never be able to look inside with humbleness. You will never be that part of your solution. It's hard to face any blame you might have. Your blame only came as a result of your abuser's blame, so it's reactionary. Find the courage to name your part in this. Only then can it be overcome. Only then can it go away.

Perhaps your behavior isn't flirtatiousness; perhaps it's control. Perhaps you refuse to give up control of anything because control was ripped from you in your past. So you hold on tenaciously, because your subconscious believes your survival depends on it. It's going to cost you relationships, jobs, and peace.

Perhaps your behavior is cruelty, or lack of compassion. Perhaps your behavior is alcoholism or substance abuse. These behaviors make sense because of what we've been through. Depending on our personalities, our abuse will manifest differently in our lives. But it *will* make defaults in your character. Leaving those defaults there means you're still giving part of your life to your abuser. It's tough, tough work, but I determined my father wasn't going to maintain ANY control over who I was and how I acted. Just think—your abuser took your past. Will you give him your future as well? Think of it as him still controlling you, and then see how strong is your desire to stop it.

Ask God what unhealthy defaults your abuse has caused. He will be kind and tender about showing you. The best part is, He will help you without condemnation. He won't use words like "blame" or "responsibility." He will simply guide you, step by small step, to better, healthier mindsets and actions. You cannot fix what you have no idea is a problem. Tell God you want to be the best possible version of yourself. Then picture yourself a chunk of clay that God is molding into a beautiful sculpture. Be willing to give things up, to change, to see things differently, as God lovingly gives you a new shape.

You've probably heard the expression "a leopard doesn't change its spots." To the world, that is true. But how glorious it is to realize that God can! Satan would want you to think that your defaults are so much a part of you, you can never get rid of them. God is the only one who can change you foundationally. Because the leopard image resonated with me, I started praying to God, "Lord, change my spots." It was an endearment between God and me that acknowledged I was asking Him for foundational change that only He could do.

Over the years, I stopped wondering if the particular spot I was working on was a result of my abuse. We are complicated creatures, and we will never know exactly what factors created or caused a behavior pattern in us. But just creating the new default of asking for God's help when we see a negative in ourselves is so healthy. Skip asking why. Get right to the important task of fixing it.

A fifth nugget is misplaced blame. Just as you accept that your abuser cannot control your actions and defaults, you must also accept that they do not control these in other men. Don't hold your abuser's sin against every man out there. The world is more aware than ever of racism, sexism, classism, ageism—every way that we can judge a person by the wrong things. You would not look at a black person and say automatically that you don't trust them just because they're black. But abuse victims often do this to men.

A man hurt you, therefore, no man is worthy of trust. This is an understandable but erroneous conclusion. Give every person the same clean slate you would want. You don't want to be judged by your gender, your past, your family, etc. Don't judge anybody else by those things. God can only give you the beautiful gift of real love if you open your heart to it. Keeping yourself "protected" by refusing to ever trust is actually keeping yourself hurt and lonely and isolated.

I'll tell you now that if you do find real love, he *will* hurt you. He won't mean to, but he's not perfect and you aren't either. If the first time your boyfriend/fiance/husband steps on your toes, you think, *See? Men are trash, he hurt me!*, then you've missed the point. You will both stumble through your journey of love, being imperfect towards each other and sometimes hurting the other, but also loving the other into a place of peace, comfort, and joy that is a true gift of God.

I did not suffer this particular point. I went the other way and trusted everybody. I credited every man out there with the ability to love away my hurts. Of course they didn't. I didn't have maturity or wisdom, and I certainly didn't have healthy boundaries. My hurt caused me to look in the wrong places. I didn't apply any standards. I allowed anybody in, anybody who seemed to take a shine to me. Don't go this way either!

It is important that we learn to see men properly. We must ask God to help us adjust the filter through which we see men. The filter of abuse causes us to credit them with the wrong attributes—we either assume they're bad when they're not, or we assume they're good when they're not. Normal people apply Godly filters and use standards to sift out who they are going to get into a relationship with. We need to ask God for those unblemished filters.

Most of us don't try to get revenge on our abuser. We want to stay as far away as possible, and we don't spend our time plotting evil ways to destroy them. But what we do is treat other men poorly because of them. Understanding misplaced blame will help us avoid doing that. Understanding God's sense of justice will help us avoid doing that as well.

God says He is our vindicator. He is in charge of meting out revenge. He makes it clear that we are not to. If we truly understand this, we will not fall into the trap of many abuse victims, and treat men badly. *No other man can pay you back for what your abuser did.* Make sure you aren't subconsciously asking them to.

Know that you may not see God's justice. We love the Hollywood movies where the good guy wins in the end and the bad guy definitely gets his comeuppance. It satisfies a sense of justice that most of us have as human beings. God put that there, and He knows we long for justice. Our souls crave it, and for good reasons. But can we leave it in God's hands? Can we trust Him when we don't see it happening? Well, we have to.

We are told right from the beginning that we won't understand how God does things. We have to be ok with that. He is the creator, He is in charge. We are the creation, we are not in charge. It's easy to get that fact when it's just generalities, but we get tripped up when we take it down to the level of details—when we don't see God doing what we think He should. Apply your trust in God. He says He will hand out justice. Leave it completely with Him, and free yourself of the need to see it happen. Trust means knowing God means what He says. Rest in that. Cut the ties and leave your abuser in God's hands.

This brings up another point I struggled with for years. We don't want to think of our abuser as getting God's forgiveness. If our abuser isn't saved, we don't want them to give their hearts to God and receive that amazing gift of salvation that they don't deserve. We want them to burn in hell and suffer, not get to heaven right beside us, freed from their sin by forgiveness.

I touched on this in a previous chapter, but I want to look deeper at it here.

We understand us forgiving them, because it frees us. But picturing God completely forgiving them can turn into an ugly ball of wax. Having their heinous crime lost forever in the sea of God's forgetfulness, just like our sins are? That's a hard one to swallow. At least it was for me. We want God to deal with them, we trust God for pure justice. But the forgiveness and freedom part, true happiness and joy flowing from their hearts, is not something that is easy to picture.

If your abuser came to your church, all cleaned up, in a suit and tie, humbled and smiling, and gave a special presentation about how God had saved him from a wretched life of sin, would you be happy for him? Or would you want the entire congregation to know what he did, what an awful sinner he was, what a hypocrite he was? Would your soul cry out that he didn't deserve a nice, cleaned-up life?

What if that was God's justice?

When we leave something in God's hands, our trust in Him has to be absolute. When we hand over our ashes and get beauty in return, we cut the ties to that whole bundle of garbage. We leave it with God, and essentially give Him permission to do whatever He wants with it. Once you throw away your kitchen trash bags every day, do you care what happens to them? Do you instruct the garbage men what to do with them? Of course not. We leave our emotional garbage with God with the same sense of freedom.

Know then, that God rejoices in every single saved life, and that includes your abuser.

You may not ever have to deal with this part of it. But I don't want it to derail you if you come face to face with it. I don't want your healing journey to depend on the fact that your abuser's "justice" got meted out according to your desires and your plan.

God does give us an idea of how He handles justice. In fact, He tells us to use the very same method. I have said it before, but it is so important that it definitely bears repeating. God says to overcome evil with good. We can never beat evil with evil. We could never make our abuser pay by abusing him. We could never see him suffer enough to overcome what he did to us. The only way to truly overcome it is to fight it with good.

It doesn't make sense to our logical mind. And it certainly doesn't feel right. But here is another example of having to trust God and His word. Do we really believe Him? Our healing depends on us answering yes to that question. *Let God fix your abuser with good.*

One thing I have never understood about abuse is how the abused become the abusers. It's a sickening thought. How on earth could an abuse victim turn around and do to someone else the awful things that were done to them? They *know* how horrific it feels to be on the receiving end. They know how the effects of even one instance can last forever. They know how their victim's soul will scream that she is innocent and undeserving, and how part of her will die under the cruel injustice. So how could they possibly perpetrate what was done to them?

I do not have answers, but the evidence of it happening is overwhelming. You need only to read the news to hear time and time again that a criminal was discovered to have had an abusive past. If your defaults lean at all to expressing your anger and pain by perpetuating your abuse, you need to desperately seek God with every fiber of your being. I will just reiterate that God can heal such defaults the same way he can heal lesser ones like flirtatiousness or extreme submissiveness. He does it through our willingness to be changed, our desire to know our faults and correct them, and our willingness to repeatedly experience and respond to God's conviction that will lead us away from harmful thoughts and actions.

My father was a Christian, truly a man of God. And not only did he sexually abuse his children, he also had an affair for several years. He hurt my mother terribly, and almost ended their marriage. But he was a born-again Christian! His sins were so grievous, the pain of them had the power to destroy lives. I remember at times almost wanting the "comfort" of believing that he would rot in hell. But I knew he would not. He was saved, and would spend eternity in heaven, despite what he did to his three children and his wife.

That was really hard to wrap my mind around. A couple things helped me. One is that God's mercy is incredible. It feels a lot better when that mercy is directed at me, but still the power of it is undeniable. The amazing gift of eternal life in heaven is ours just for believing, not for behaving well.

The second thing that helped me was to look at the Biblical David. He was so important and influential that only Jesus is talked about more than him in the Bible. David was described as a man after God's own heart. God is quoted as saying that David is a man who will do the work of the Lord, fully embrace the Lord's plans, and fulfill the Lord's desires. Doesn't it make you wonder, when David's sins are among the worst we can think of? He committed adultery and murder. He stole a man's wife and then had that man killed. Yet, that is not how God defined him. David was defined by his heart.

The world will not see us as God does. He tells us not to judge each other because He is the only one who can see our hearts. All we can see is our actions. We cannot help but notice actions and draw conclusions, but we must remember that God always has the final say. David's life is a testimony to what really matters to God.

And my father's name is David.

God never wastes your pain. That may sound strange, but it's another way of saying that He can turn everything into something good. Let Him. Be an active participant by doing everything you can. Know that you are partners with God in your healing process. He won't do your part, and you can't do His.

If you stay parked at the point of your pain, you will feel its negative effects forever. You have that right. God will never force a solution on you. But if you are willing to leave it behind, to forgive, to let go of resentment, to hope for something better, to let God in and break apart the strongholds of hate, He will turn your pain into something good. You will discover victory and strength and joy and peace like you've never known. Don't waste your pain. God won't.

As a final tidbit—stop hating your abuser and start loving God. Our emotions have power and energy. It's technically true that the opposite of hate is love. But when it comes to letting go of hate and disentangling our lives from its oppressive hold, the opposite of hate is neutrality. That is what we are aiming for here. I am not telling you to love your abuser. But every time you feel hate towards him, love on God. Tell God how much you love Him. Tell God everything you are thankful for. Sing a praise song to God. Don't concentrate on not hating your abuser. Rather, concentrate on loving God. Love will push out hate.

And when your healing is complete, you will be left with two amazing things: a love for God that has been nurtured properly, and an absence of hate towards your abuser. You will reach that blessed place of neutrality, where your abuser cannot evoke negative emotions in you and send you on a roller coaster that ends in despair. The peace and joy of a strong relationship with God will be with you every moment of every day, and Satan can throw his best darts at you by bringing up your past and all your pain, and it will have no effect on you anymore.

Lord, I want to constantly move onward and upward in my healing journey. Help me to understand that my feelings are not facts. Thank you that your truth is stronger than anything I may be feeling at the moment. Help me to choose to declare your truth to overcome my feelings. I acknowledge you, Lord, as the master architect. Thank you that you promise to work all things together for good. Help me to believe that, and trust you to do it. Help me to have a proper perspective on my abuser's actions. My abuser was not happy but I know I can be. He was hurting, but I choose to overcome my hurt. Though it's a tough process, I want to know what negative defaults I have in my life right now that I can change. Show me things I can fix, and then help me fix them. Help me not to blame other men for my abuser's actions. I acknowledge that no other man can pay me back for what he did. Help me to remove any faulty filters through which I see men, and help me to act in a wise and godly way towards them. Lord I trust you for justice. I put my abuser in your hands, and completely leave him there. In Jesus' name, amen.

Chapter 10—God and Sex: Never The Twain Shall Meet?

It seems obvious that, as a survivor of sexual abuse, you were taught to view sex wrongly. I always knew that. But still, it took me years into my healing journey before I embraced it fully, before I actually attempted to work on the task of *connecting* God and sex.

Because I desperately wanted to be a wife, I prayed right from the beginning that God would help me see sex as healthy and good. I wanted to picture a penis without accompanying violent images. I wanted to embrace all that sex had to offer without feeling like it was dirty or compromised. And I did pray for these things.

But my love life was the one area where I stumbled the most.

Even after I felt like I had achieved a lot of healing, I didn't understand why I would mess up the one thing that meant the most to me. I was determined to not play the victim, and so I didn't blame Dad for my actions. I took full responsibility, and then felt the huge frustration of breaking my own heart with my behaviors.

God had to first bring me to a complete acceptance and understanding of being my own solution before He could reveal to me what would have otherwise sent me off a cliff of anger. I had to fully embrace the truth that "It doesn't matter how I got this way, this is how I am." I stated it over and over, and then one day, it hit me. That's the only way to explain it.

One day, I was thinking about it and a huge peace settled into my heart. It felt like a warm blanket. I truly didn't care who or what caused me to be like this; I only wanted to get better. God's Word was true—stating and believing something comes first. Then the feeling of it, that makes it seem real, comes afterwards.

It was only then that God could gently show me that Dad had wired me wrong. I could look at actual causes without my emotions sending me into a tailspin. I was at the point where I could look at reasons, not blame. There is a huge difference. When you are free from the desire to blame, and ready to be 100% of your own solution, you can objectively look at root causes.

I was able to see that I had given every other area of my life over to God except romance. And there was a trail of faith landmarks to prove it. I trusted God completely with my work life, my health, my friends and family relationships, my hobbies and dreams. And He was faithful to show through in all those areas. But my love life was a train wreck. It wasn't that I consciously decided not to trust God. I just lived like I didn't. I made foolish decisions with hurtful consequences, and kept telling myself I'd be ok.

When God peeled back the layers, there were a lot of reasons to be ragingly angry at Dad. He was indeed responsible for the foundation of my personality, upon which I tried so hard to build a good life. Had I not been secure in the truths I've discussed so far in this book, I would have fallen apart with grief over the person I could have been.

As a baby, we all have millions of neurons in our brain. What experience teaches us is how to connect them. We connect simple truths like eating food makes us feel good, blankets keep us warm, crying gets us attention, Mom is a source of security. Imagine the faulty connections cemented in our brains when love is connected to fear and revulsion, happiness is connected to phoniness and secrecy, and sex is connected to shame and pain.

Repeated experiences, year after year, solidified these connections. It's like the software of my brain was being written, and after all my brain development was done, I simply followed the "program" life had given me. To simplify, if my brain was a calculator, I kept punching in 5x2= and kept getting 12 as a result. I prayed against the 12, I called it down in Jesus' name, I declared that it wasn't the truth, I dutifully tried to fight it. I stated over and over that 10 is what I wanted. Then I would again find myself in a situation where I figuratively punched in 5x2=. And there was that darn 12.

God was finally able to show me that I had to rewire my calculator. I had to take it apart and actually switch the wires to make new connections. That is how foundational abuse is. If you had repeated abuse during your formative years, *you are wired wrong.*

I pictured thousands, maybe millions of neural connections in my brain that were faulty. My actual brain was a mess. I remember having gone to a homeopathic doctor when I was 40 because of severe stomach pains that traditional medicine had been unable to diagnose. This doctor hooked me up to a machine that she said would pick up on my body's energy and give her a full description of what was going on. I sat there for 10 minutes with wires connected to me, praying into the silence, wondering what the machine would spit out.

Sure enough, she instantly diagnosed my problem as excessive candida, and gave me a solution. But the most striking part of that experience was when she was looking at the readout from the machine. She very calmly said, "I see that you had extreme trauma in your childhood." She professionally didn't say anything else, and because my racing brain couldn't come up with a response, neither did I. But it hit me like a ton of bricks. Decades later, my abuse still showed in my tissues. Not just in my emotions or in my thoughts, but my physical cells were emanating an energy that showed trauma.

At the time, I didn't dig into it. I was in too much physical pain from the candida problem, and was given a natural rather than pharmaceutical solution. So it took weeks to fix rather than days. It wasn't until several years later that God allowed the magnitude of it to settle in. I was wired wrong.

It wasn't that I didn't trust God. It was that my initial neural connections taught me that God was on the outside. And sex was on the inside. God was in the polished, candy-coated image we had to show the world. God was in the prayers we prayed as a family—about jobs, health, moving houses, etc. God was in the conspicuous things, the innocent things we were allowed to talk about.

But God wasn't in those awful sexual things on the inside. The deep hidden yucky things that caused the pain weren't touched by God. We never prayed about those things. We were spanked for other sins that God would disapprove of, but there was no punishment for these ones. We were expected to adhere to a strict moral code because God was the source of right and wrong. Except for what Dad was doing to us—we weren't supposed to question the morality of that. We were taught that God cared about all aspects of our lives. Except this one. We weren't to ever talk about this one.

All of my initial neural connections separated God from sex.

The only part of it that had morality attached was in keeping silent—we were told it was right to keep silent and wrong to tell. So guess how my first sexual experiences played out? They were with the wrong people, done in secrecy, and kept hidden. I wasn't consciously repeating the pattern. But in hindsight, I realized that I fully expected God would bless me as I lived every other part of my life for Him. I didn't realize the huge damage I was doing by continuing to keep this one part "on the inside."

Then I railed against myself in guilt. How could I do these things? How could I commit sins I knew were so bad? What on earth was wrong with me?

It is amazing how powerful are the defaults we create in our formative years. My love and faith in God were making me try so hard to get that 10 on my calculator, and I was crying broken hearted tears every time that 12 showed up.

I had to connect God and sex.

I thought I already had. And don't get me wrong—all the steps leading up to this were healthy and necessary. Don't worry if you've been praying against the 12 on your calculator. We need to get upset enough at the darn 12's to put in the effort required to rewire our calculators! But I realized I saw God more in every other part of life than sex. Other areas of life could have their bad parts—financial hardship, bullies, not getting the promotion, scary surgeries needed, arguments with loved ones—but nothing matched the disgusting shame of sex done wrongly.

And so a loving God slowly got separated from the sewage where sex dwelt in my soul.

It is often more constructive to concentrate your energies on creating new habits rather than breaking old ones. A habit that is starved will eventually die. One that is fed will eventually grow. So in addition to praying against my bad defaults, I started praying FOR new connections.

I actually prayed for my brain to be rewired. I read a story one time about a prostitute who had found Jesus and prayed for restoration. God actually renewed her physically, back to the point of being virginal. God wants to heal every part of us! Knowing how completely your abuse damaged you allows you to pray more specifically and effectively, as well as allows you to appreciate the full scope of how much you've overcome.

I told God I wanted sex to belong to Him just as much as every other aspect of my life did. So I had to face my views on sex. All of them.

God created sex. It is entirely His invention. It isn't something dirty that the enemy snuck in. It is an amazing gift meant to be pleasurable in the extreme. He gave it immense power to bond a man and a woman. It deserves an elevated place in our hearts and minds. We may have to manually elevate it there if life has left it in the sewers for us. And the best way to do that is to see God all over it.

Have you ever pictured God right there while you're having sex? For years, it seemed dirty for me to do so, even though in my head I knew God had created it. It was so comforting for me to envision God right with me, as His Word says He is, in every other path of life. But in the bedroom, somehow God was waiting outside the door instead.

There is no shame automatically inherent in sex. It is private, and its beauty depends on it remaining so. But that's different than shame. God didn't give us something that we automatically have to work at removing the bad parts of. What God gave us is something totally completely and inherently beautiful. Just like free will, individual people can choose to use it badly. But that is no reflection on God or His gift.

Sex is a huge blessing. It is not meant to just be endured or tolerated. It is meant to be embraced and thoroughly enjoyed. God likes seeing us enjoy it. Imagine that! Far from keeping God respectfully out of your sex life, start thanking God for sex. Allow yourself to picture God with you in your bedroom. It may seem uncomfortable at first. But you need to let God reclaim that part. He is not trying to intrude on your privacy or intimacy. He just needs to be connected to sex. I would not recommend trying to think about God during all of your sexual encounters. I would only suggest you do this as an interim chapter on your healing journey. As you are praying that God rewires your brain, show Him you are serious by deliberately participating in that rewiring.

We have learned that declaring the truth of things has power. We have learned that doing that often comes before feeling it. So pick up that spiritual tool in this case too. State out loud, "God made sex." "Sex is meant to be enjoyable." "God wants me to like sex." One of my favorites is, "Sex is amazing and beautiful." God's Word will not return to Him void. Stating and believing these truths will eventually produce the feeling of it. Defaults change with determination and repetition. Determine that you will replace shame and ugliness with joy and beauty.

I would encourage you to follow this one all the way to highest victory. Many people content themselves with stopping at neutrality. If they can just get sex to not hurt and shame them, they are happy. They brought it up from the ditches into "real life" and cut away its negative ties. That is huge progress. But don't stop there! That is like seeing your child unwrap a present that fell in the dirt. The dirty wrapping paper is now gone. But how sad it would be if your child never took the toy out and played with it. Don't settle for mediocre when God wants fantastic.

Sex is in its own category of pleasure and it is physical, mental, and emotional. Nothing compares to it. Don't leave its potential untapped. Pray that God would open up its entire world to you. God doesn't give gifts halfway. If you acknowledge that God is the source and creator of sex, that

He meant it entirely for good, and that He is happy when you are enjoying it, then there is no reason not to reach for its highest experiences.

There is another aspect to viewing sex properly. If you want to enjoy something to the fullest, you have to follow the instructions. Sex has boundaries. Everything good in life does. We cannot hold it against God that He dictated boundaries on sex. And we cannot expect to get the most out of it if we go outside those boundaries.

Sex has a proper context. It goes more and more against the popular world view as the world gets more "progressive." We must accept that the truth outlined in the Bible does not depend on cultural norms. We must respect that God said sex is to be done in marriage, between a man and a woman. Within those healthy boundaries, sex is a world of pleasure that can brighten your life exponentially. Outside of those healthy boundaries, no matter how much you are determined to enjoy it, sex has the ability to hurt you incredibly.

If you are reading this book, you or a loved one have probably already been hurt by sex. You have already seen the damage done when its boundaries are defied. Again, don't just fix that by going halfway. Don't tell yourself that you will only have sex in loving relationships, or when it is your choice. If it's outside of marriage, then it is still outside of God's rules. Go all the way with sex. Let God show you what He meant sex to be by experiencing it in the way He intended. I don't know about you, but I sure tried it my way. God was compassionate and understanding as I stumbled and bumbled my way through trying to make sex good. But

I would never have reached that goal if I didn't also respect God's boundaries.

Similarly, don't put boundaries on sex that God didn't put there. Be creative! And allow your spouse to be. If your abuser "got creative," perhaps you have closed your mind's door to the possibilities of imaginative sex. Don't let your abuser deprive you! Remember that everything you cut off in your future because of your abuser is like handing him part of you that you should never be giving him.

I am not saying that you can't have limits. You certainly can. The marriage relationship should be a safe place to express and explore them. Mutual respect of each other's boundaries is essential. I am not advocating for letting a spouse be sexually dominant and making you uncomfortable, just because it's within a marriage. In the context of your healing journey, this chapter assumes you are dealing with healthy sex in the *aftermath* of abuse. Do not allow abuse to continue in the marriage bedroom!

But don't go the other way, taking the path of least resistance, and thereby depriving yourself. I have heard Christian couples say that anything other than missionary position is wrong. God never said that. God gave us a world of pleasure possibilities in sex. If you decline certain sexual activities because they are uncomfortable, that is fine. But don't decline them because you think they are wrong.

Sex is a world too easily defiled. We know the truth of that all too well. But our healing journey must include every effort to turn that around. It is hard to open yourself to something that hurt you so badly. It may seem easier to heal from the hurt and then never let the hurtful thing near you again. But I want to see you go all the way to complete victory! Your future shouldn't just hold the absence of pain; it should also hold the presence of pleasure. Your abuse made it harder for you to get it, but you have the tools and it is there for the taking. Start looking forward to sex being a source of incredible joy!

Lord, thank you that you made sex, and it is a beautiful gift from you to us. I pray that you rewire my brain in a way that connects sex to you. I don't want sex to be something outside of my relationship with you. I surrender the negative ways I see sex, and I open my heart and mind to your healthy and godly definitions and boundaries instead. Please redo the neural connections in my body that were wrongly wired in my past. I want you to be just as much a part of my sex life as you are of the other parts of my life. I acknowledge that though sex was used in the past to hurt me, sex done within your boundaries is immensely pleasurable. Please show me sex the way you intended it. Please help me to participate in sex to the fullest capacity of my enjoyment. In Jesus' name, amen.

Chapter 11 —Grace, Gratitude, and Growth

God's grace really is amazing. It is automatically a part of who He is and what He does. But it deserves recognition on its own. We have talked about tools we can use on our healing journey; grace is a tool God uses. Gifts, favor, mercy, power—all of these are summed up in grace. It is a unique way for God to bless his children, to fix lives, to provide endless second chances, to right the impossible wrongs. Every time He uses it on us or for us, our lives are improved because of it. There is no substitute for it. God is the only source of grace, and it's more generous and powerful than you can imagine.

Power is indeed a big part of the definition of grace. God will empower you. It is supernatural. It does not have to fit into the limits of understanding of your human mind and intellect. It is all wrapped up in this beautiful gift that God wants to give you, whether you understand it or not. When you pray for help, and are willing to take even the smallest baby step on your healing journey, then believe that you have it. You have grace on your side. You have incredible power from the creator of the universe, working through the details of your life to bring you to a better place.

Let the power of grace work its way through your thoughts, your words, and your actions. It won't feel like an instant magic wand fix. God wants to build permanent habits in your heart and mind just like exercising builds up a muscle, so it takes time. Every time you wait that split second before saying something negative about yourself, your future, or your abuser, and then decide not to, grace has empowered you. Every time you discover your thoughts ruminating over the horrid memories you have, and you deliberately distract yourself with other thoughts or do something different, grace has empowered you. Every time you offer the sacrifice of praise and give worship to God whether you feel like it or not, grace has empowered you.

Grace will systemically change your defaults. Grace can give you patience where you didn't have any. Grace can soften your tongue and put gentler words in your mouth. Grace can make you kind where you used to be harsh. Grace can temper your pride and guide you towards humbleness. When I was praying, "God, change my spots," I was welcoming the power of grace to do more than I was humanly capable of myself.

Grace is more than just power though. It's an incredible gift! Grace is undeserved favor. Grace is being given things you didn't earn. Your abuse was undeserved. Grace is undeserved as well, only in the opposite direction. How long have you spent fixated on an undeserved negative? Start fixating on an undeserved positive! God wants to give you fabulous things. Open your heart to receive them. It is a good idea to start keeping a prayer journal. Record every time a prayer is answered, or an unexpected blessing came your way. That is grace. That is God reaching into your life and touching your circumstances. That is God being a loving father and gifting things to you that only He can.

Grace comes in so many forms, it would be impossible to list them. That is part of why it is so wonderful—it is personal. The Bible tells us that every good thing comes from God. Have you noticed them? Or do you overlook them? We must believe God's Word, and so we must accept that God is constantly doing good things for us. Grace can come in your work life, your personal relationships, your health, your children, your finances, your hobbies. There is no area of your life that God is not interested in blessing. God can open doors for you and close doors for you. Both are grace.

I have found myself thanking God that I remembered some small thing at the last minute, or a traffic light turned green right when I needed it, or I found something I had lost, or the grocery store had the exotic product I was looking for. The list is endless. God's grace is beautiful and abundant. If we choose to focus on it, our joy will be multiplied and we will feel so much closer to God.

I was feeling lonely and sad one day, while standing on the top deck of a cruise ship. I won't go into the details of how a sad mindset could plague me in such a beautiful setting, but I will say God hears our cries no matter our circumstances. I told God I needed a hug. I needed something personal from Him. And so I asked God to please have a whale jump in front of me. I stared out at that endless expanse of water, and chose to see God in it. And right then, a whale jumped. It didn't just breach, it jumped completely, full body, out of the water. It landed with a tremendous splash. The tears flowed down my cheeks and shivers covered my skin as I felt God hugging me, exactly the way I had asked Him. How amazing is God! How loving and generous is His grace, to give us gifts like that!

I have beat out 400 other people for a job I wanted. I was given my dream home, after driving by it for three years and never imagining it could ever be mine. I was deemed a medical "write off" when my appendix burst and I laid there for 10 hours afterwards, unconscious and thoroughly poisoned, and God prompted the doctor to do the surgery anyway and fully healed me. I was in a Suburban that got hit by a van on an interstate going highway speed, and because I wasn't wearing a seatbelt, I hit the sides and roof multiple times as the vehicle flipped and rolled over and over. I walked away without a single scratch or bruise. I have so many examples of God's grace in my life. All good things come from God. We need to see that, and believe it. No matter what atrocities we have endured, God has not forgotten about us. Make a point of noticing God's grace in your life. It is such a wonderful feeling.

Taking our focus off of what is bad and hurtful and unjust, and putting it onto what is good and helpful and loving causes a significant change in our hearts. It brings about gratitude. Gratitude is one of the proven characteristics of happy people. God explains that in His word, but it makes me smile that the worldly sector has reached the same conclusion through research and studies.

Gratitude is something we can choose to have. It's not dependent on good things happening to us. But it is difficult when something as tragic as abuse is hovering over our lives. Sometimes it takes the mental energy of switching our focus onto the evidence of God's grace before we can summon up some gratitude. Gratitude then becomes a door through which more grace can pour into our lives.

It is almost impossible to be truly grateful and bitter at the same time. One pushes the other one out. Thankfully, it is our choice as to which one that is. We do not have to wait until we feel like we won a lottery before we can be thankful. We can choose to look around and notice the things that deserve gratitude. The great thing is, they exist right alongside of the things that can drag us down.

Life will never be all good or all bad. So if we are waiting for all the negatives to disappear before we show gratitude, we will never get there. We have to purposely make an effort to let the good shine stronger. Just like a camera, our minds will "develop" whatever we focus on. There could be a beautiful rose blooming just inches away from a steaming pile of cow manure. Moving the "camera lens" of your mind just a few inches will determine whether you are focusing on something good or something bad, the rose or the manure. We should rejoice in the fact that we get to choose. It is especially victorious for abuse victims who had their choices taken away, to realize areas of life, even small ones, where choice is indeed ours.

If you are not used to thanking God, you may need to start a new habit. If you have spent a lifetime stewing in the juices of resentment and injustice, then finding reasons to be thankful will not come naturally. It is human nature to allow negativity to run rampant. Or rather, it happens without us even trying. Overcoming the sinful human nature to show the fruits of the spirit takes effort. If we allow ourselves to feel whatever the world throws at us, and then allow those feelings to dictate our mindsets and moods, we will never naturally be thankful.

So start making the effort to notice God's grace in your life. Then determine you will be thankful for it. Start with the big things. Even if you don't feel it, say it out loud. Thank

God if you have a roof over your head, a car to drive, food to eat, and clothes on your back. Thank God if you have a spouse, children, a job, good health, enough money to pay your bills. Then move on to smaller things. Thank God if you have entertainment in your life—watching a movie, playing golf, having friends over, enjoying a glass of wine. The list is truly endless. I even find myself thanking God for hot water when I'm enjoying a particularly relaxing shower, because for a year my family didn't have running water and we had to bathe in a very cold lake. Nothing is too big or small to thank God for.

God needs our gratitude. At least this is something we can relate to. We want to give our children good things too. But how sad would it be if our children never thanked us. We deliberately give gifts on special occasions, but we give countless other times just to make our children happy. A vacation they really wanted, a toy they have been admiring for months, an ice cream treat, pizza for dinner instead of something healthy, a sleepover party, a new iPhone—an immeasurable number of things we give our children because we love seeing them happy. God is the same way with us. Don't leave Him out of the equation. We can fully understand why He would want our gratitude. Let's make sure we give it to Him.

Do not let the fact that something bad happened to you keep you from giving God gratitude. Remember that your child might break a leg playing in the back yard, despite your best efforts at protection. That does not mean your child shouldn't be thankful for everything else you've given him. You want your child to be able to run and play and exercise his body, and also make decisions and use his mind and morals. But to do that, you have to give him freedom to possibly hurt himself. God treats us much the same as we treat our children in this way, so we have a natural means of understanding Him. God is not to blame for the bad things that happened to you. But He is the giver of all the good things that are yours.

Your past is not going to go away. So you have the choice of letting it dictate your mindset, or letting other factors weigh in. Picture a balance scale. Your abuse is on one side. If you never put anything on the other side to counterbalance, the abuse would always weigh heaviest. The reality of that would be that you would always be unhappy. You would likely be resentful, bitter, unforgiving, and angry too. I realize you didn't put the abuse there. And you cannot remove it. But you have the amazing ability to outbalance it! All you have to do is put enough things on the other side of the balance scale to weigh heavier than the negative.

That is where gratitude becomes so important. Acknowledging that something is good enough to be placed on that other side of the scale most often happens when we decide to be grateful. You have probably heard "count your blessings" many times. Well, you can't count them if you don't even know they are there. An attitude of gratitude will open your eyes to all the blessings you do have. Then as you count them, and are truly thankful for them, they are heaped onto that other side of the balance scale. Pretty soon they outweigh the abuse. After years of a thankful lifestyle, the abuse is such a small thing, that even though you couldn't remove it, it does not factor in to your level of peace and happiness.

This is one way we can fight evil with good. It's been repeated many times, so hopefully it is sinking in. It's not just a battle slogan—there are many ways we can put action behind it and actually accomplish it in our lives. Gratitude is one way. There is no way we could outweigh abuse on that balance scale by only having other negatives to work with. The only way is to allow the positives to pile up.

Every time you take even the smallest step in the right direction, you are growing. The world does not ask you to do this. Remember, as we discussed earlier, the world gives you a constant crutch, and a constant pity party. You have every logical reason, according to the humanness of the world, to stay where you are. Parked at the point of your pain. Permanently camped in "woe is me" land. Or even worse, falling further and further into despair because of the horrible things that happened to you. The world may wish you healing and growth, the same way a Hallmark card might. But only God has the power to truly give it to you.

God does ask you to grow. God loves you too much to leave you the way you are. Stagnation was never part of God's plan. He has an onward and upward victorious path for every part of our lives that we hand over to Him. In recognizing that you are on a journey, made up of an endless number of tiny steps, make sure to give yourself gratitude too. Look at how far you have come, rather than how far you have to go. Keep a prudent, healthy perspective on your goals, but acknowledge progress. We need that. Even if you look back and only see five baby steps, be happy! Those are five steps to the good. Those are five nails in the coffin of Satan's plans to keep you down. Those are five reasons to thank God and believe in the hope He has for you. And those are five steps better than you were before you took them.

One thing you are probably noticing about the tools, the battles, and the progress, is that it's all in our minds. God is not asking you to go build cities, or run marathons, or organize missions, or start huge companies. There is nothing physical about the grace, gratitude, and growth we are talking about here. Lest you think it's daunting and you are too exhausted, you could do these lessons, and take these steps every day, just sitting on your couch. All these victories start in your THOUGHTS—you have to decide, in your mind, to do them. It is that simple.

Your thoughts are more powerful than you realize. But once you do realize that truth, you can start weaponizing them for the good. You are not a victim of every thought that pops into your head. You get to decide if that thought stays there. You also get to decide to deliberately think about other things. Just changing your thought patterns is growth. You can give yourself credit for progress, rather amazing progress actually, if you can exercise even a small amount of control over your thoughts. Think about what you are thinking about!

The Bible says we are to renew our minds daily. Get that—every single day, our minds need renewing. Obviously God knew how He made us and He knew that we would need to deliberately address our thoughts, constantly. How do we renew our minds? Think of it as a simple exchange: out with the bad, in with the good.

Learn to cast down bad thoughts. Do not dwell on your past pain. That would derail anyone. If you spend time going over and over the cruelty and injustice, you will feel down, you will act down, you will BE down. You will never reap happiness thoughts if you sow depressing thoughts. So do not dwell on your past! You are not to blame if bad thoughts come to your mind. But kick them out when they do, over and over. Think of them knocking at the door of your mind. Decide you are not going to answer the door.

The best way to cast out bad thoughts is to deliberately think good thoughts. You may want to make an actual list of things you can think, say, or do when a negative thought comes into your head. Perhaps you've memorized some scripture verses that you can say out loud. Perhaps you can start praying and thanking God for every blessing you can think of at that moment. Perhaps you have a favorite song you can sing out loud. Call a friend. Read the Bible. Start exercising. Make a snack. Refuse to let your mind dwell in a bad place. Rejoice in your ability to choose, and choose something good. Replacing the bad with the good will create a new habit. It may seem tedious at first, but habits build out of repetition. So be diligent in repeating.

And then notice how your life improves. It STARTS with your thoughts, but then it trickles into every other part of your life. Everything you say and do is affected by your thoughts. How much you enjoy a movie, conversation you have at a friends' get-together, what you choose to do on a day off, how often you call your parents, how you spend your money—the list of actions in your life is endless. But those actions can be enjoyable or miserable, based on your thoughts. And you may or may not even take those actions, depending on your thoughts.

I don't want you to make the mistake of thinking your words and actions don't matter. They very much do. But they are a result of your thoughts. So recognizing that the battleground is your mind, and winning the battle there, sets you up to be victorious and happy in your words and actions. Think of your words and actions as fruit—they can only grow once the fertile soil of healthy thoughts is created.

Lord, thank you so much for grace. Your grace really is amazing. Thank you for the power that is in it. Thank you for the favor and gifts that are in it. I acknowledge that grace comes from you, and I want to see it at work in my life. I have so many reasons to be thankful, despite the bad that happened to me. Help create a habit of thankfulness in me, Lord, help me to gladly show you my gratitude every day. Thank you for the ability to choose my thoughts. I realize that the battle is being fought in my mind, and I want to think the right things. Help me to take my thoughts captive, and to overcome bad ones with good ones. Thank you for your grace that helps me every step of this journey. In Jesus' name, amen.

Chapter 12 — Beautiful Pearls

You are in control of making your future infinitely better than your past. And God is your constant loving helper. Though you may stumble through unfamiliar concepts, just being willing to leave your past behind you, and embrace a future that is brighter than you ever imagined, means you will never be the cast-down victim who started reading this book.

God understands the intricacies of your personal situation like nobody else. Though I believe the wisdom in this book applies to all abuse survivors, I hope you find further encouragement in the knowledge that God does not just hand out one generic cookie-cutter path of healing to everyone. Trust that when you apply God's general principles as this book outlines, He will work out a personal and individual plan for you. Remember that God wants relationship with you! Your steps on your journey will be yours alone. Take encouragement from what He has done for others, but don't look for your exact path in another's life. Trust God to be intimately personal in how He deals with you. Your walk with God is personal—your healing with God will be too.

I now have a healthy and enjoyable relationship with my father. We don't see each other very often because we live in different countries. But when we do visit, the hugs and love are heartfelt. I do not look at him as my abuser anymore. There is good and bad in him, just like in all of us, and I am able to see the good instead of the bad. I am able to honor him as the Bible says I should. This is all thanks to

God. This is because of God's amazing and powerful ability to overcome the pain of sin, and grant me victory.

There are so many ways you will experience healing. May you smile inside every time you see that you are not the abused victim you once were. I no longer look at a penis with revulsion. I know sex is a gift from God and I can give my body wholly to my husband and enjoy it. I do not seek control, and I do not let the world walk all over me. I have a healthy backbone, and healthy boundaries. I am no longer a chameleon, giving every different audience whatever it wants from me. I love people, but I'm not tied to a people-pleasing mindset that ignores my own needs.

I see beauty in masculinity and the male sex-drive, because God made them, and they have purpose. I am no longer flirty, and I do not need validation from men in those fleeting moments of coquettish behavior. I am submissive to my husband and I want him to be a leader, but I am also a helpmate and I know I am an important equal. None of these milestones would have happened had I not willingly shed my victim mentality and embraced God's healing and God's future for me.

Don't get derailed when you need to assert your victory over again. Satan won't just leave you alone when he sees you pick up your spiritual tools. Habits are hard to break and defaults are easy to go back to. But the good news is that the solution is easy too. God didn't make it like college level calculus. It may be hard, but always remember—it's not too hard. The concepts are beautifully simple: state who you are in Christ, believe God's promises, determine to forgive, focus on the good. These can be challenging to do but they are easy to grasp in concept. Put your hand in God's and walk the whole journey, celebrating every little victory along the way. Don't get frustrated when that same "nail" appears again—be happy that you now know exactly which hammer to pick up from your tool box to pound it back down again.

I am not where I need to be. Life is a constant journey onward and upward. But thank the Lord, I'm not where I used to be. I see so much progress in my soul. The details will be different for all of you, but I trust you will see it. There will be real, tangible improvements in your life. Just the lightness you feel from cutting off the burden of baggage will make every single day better. Relationships will be easier and more rewarding. Your inner peace will be a constant comfort. Your "sacrifice of praise" will turn into a bubbling fountain of overflowing gratitude.

Let's summarize some basics for an easy and helpful visual.

When you look at the past, you see:

- It's bad.
- It wasn't your fault.
- You didn't have control.
- It can't be changed.

When you look at the future, you see:

- Endless possibilities.
- You have control.
- God has a good plan.
- Freedom to decide and choose.

Remind yourself again and again that we overcome evil with good. We can never fight evil with evil. Satan would be thrilled if you tried. Not only would you not succeed, but you'd condemn yourself to a miserable life. Only good can overcome evil. Let's break it down to simple points to help us see how the battle lines are drawn.

This is the evil that was forced into your life:

- Abuse.
- Hurt and pain.
- Emotional damage.
- Anger and hate.
- Bad habits, patterns, and defaults.
- Self-pity.
- A constant crutch/excuse to blame for your bad decisions and actions.

This is the good you use to overcome it:

- Learning to love yourself and see yourself as Christ does.
- Being grateful.
- Forgiving.
- Praying for your enemies.
- Identifying bad habits and fixing them.
- Taking responsibility for your future.
- Asking and believing for God's help.

Freedom from your past doesn't mean never having to deal with it again. Don't get derailed if a negative memory or feeling crops up. Freedom means understanding it, what it is, and knowing how to handle it. It doesn't mean you won't ever face it again; it means it won't control you. Freedom means knowing God is on your side, and your healing is entirely possible. Freedom means you are determined to ignore your setbacks and keep at it, keep at it, keep at it! Freedom from your past is the amazing tool you will use to build a beautiful future.

Keep in mind that God does not want to just bring you up to the point of normalcy. He wants to give you an abundant life. Remember that He is a God of justice. Just as we believe Him for proper punishment or recompense for our abusers, so we also believe Him for justice rewards for us. He gives us encouraging promises in His Word that He wants to repay us for the awfulness we went through. In Isaiah, He tells us that, "Instead of your shame, you will receive a double portion, and instead of disgrace, you will rejoice in your inheritance." He tells us in Joel that "I will restore to you the years that the locust has eaten", and in Jeremiah he reiterates, "I will restore health to you and heal your wounds."

He doesn't want you to be a big bundle of scar tissue. He wants you to be fully healed, victoriously enjoying life. He will restore what any human took from you, and the wonderful news is that He has more to offer us than any human can.

I understand this journey is hard. But I believe in you! I know you can do it. It's painful. But so is staying the way you are. There is pain in changing, and there is pain in never changing. One is far worse. Embrace your progress. Feel the pain of tired abs because you did the sit-ups, not the pain of bruises you received because someone hit you.

Believe me when I say it will get better. It will get easier. Joy will be bigger. The Bible tells us that "the path of the righteous grows brighter and brighter". Do you dare to believe it?

There are powerful prayers at the end of each chapter in this book. Say them out loud. Over and over. Go back as many times as you need, and repeat those life-changing power-filled words. Say them through tears. Say them even when you don't feel them. You don't need to be creative or expressive—just read those prayers out loud. God hears every word, every time. He will respond.

Take back your pearls. Your pearls of being a beautiful person. Your pearls of self-confidence and self-worth. Your pearls of future hopes and dreams. Your pearls of fulfilling sexuality. Your pearls of freedom from emotional bondage. Picture every little baby step you take on this journey as adding one more pearl to your necklace. You are working towards something incredible. The effort you are putting in is so important. God is your biggest cheerleader, and He is waiting right there to applaud your last step and help you on the next step.

You are nobody's victim. You are a child of the King. You are not used up and defiled. You have a wonderful future. You are not locked into a lesser or lower life because of what someone else did to you. You have every opportunity and every potential because of what God did for you.

Beautiful child of God—take back your pearls!

www.ingramcontent.com/pod-product-compliance
Lightning Source LLC
Chambersburg PA
CBHW070458100426
42743CB00010B/1675